any question
answered

P

PROFILE BOOKS

First published in Great Britain in 2007 by
Profile Books Ltd
3a Exmouth House
Pine Street
Exmouth Market
London EC1R 0JH
www.profilebooks.com

A CIP catalogue record for this book is available
from the British Library.

ISBN 978 1 84668 082 3

Text design by Sue Lamble
Typeset in Clarendon by MacGuru Ltd
info@macguru.org.uk

Printed and bound in the UK by
CPI Bookmarque, Croydon, CR0 4TD

contents

acknowledgements

The founders of AQA 63336 want to say a big 'thank you' to two groups of people that really matter.

Firstly, our customers: your questions continue to amaze and entertain us. Without you this book could not have happened.

Secondly, our researchers: without your hard work, attention to detail, and efforts at putting a wow into every answer our customers wouldn't come back for more, and we wouldn't have answered over 9 million questions.

foreword

Well, here it is. The difficult second book. You
may remember AQA 63336's debut, *The End of
the Question Mark*. That was a veritable feast
of questions and answers. This is no different,
apart from the fact that the questions and
answers are all different. There's a never-
ending well of queries out there and – if we can
stay with the underground theme for a moment
– we're a bottomless pit of answers. Good,
illuminating answers from human beings with
wit and style.

As you'll see, this time round we had a little
help from some of our celebrity fans. In fact we
seem to be popular with people from all walks
of life. Already in our short lives we've
answered over 9 million questions. Ask one
yourself. Save 63336 in your mobile and text us
whatever's been puzzling you (£1 per text) or
ask one for free at www.aqa.63336.com.

But enough of this foreword business. Let's get
into the nitty-gritty of what the British public
really want to know.

AQA: Any Question Answered. Says it all, really.

if I want to stuff my bra which cereal is best?

Advice and help in sex, love and life

? how would you say 'I love you' in binary code

I love you in binary code is: 01001001 (I); 01101100 (l); 01101111 (o); 01110110 (v); 01100101 (e); 01111001 (y); 01101111 (o); 01110101 (u).

? could u please tell me any baby girls' names that have the meaning mermaid

Female names which mean 'mermaid' include 'Sirena' (Chamoru Spanish), 'Azinza' (African) and 'Kyrenia' (from Cyprus).

? what would u call 9 siblings born on the same day eg 3 = triplets

The term for 9 offspring is nonuplets. The term for 6 offspring is sextuplets, 7 are known as septuplets, while 8 offspring are called octuplets.

? what is the official name of someone who loves beards

A pogonophile is someone who is fond of or who loves beards. Pogonomania is an excessive desire to have a beard or an obsession with men with beards.

? in michigan a man owns all of his wife's what

In Michigan, a man legally owns his wife's hair, and a woman is not allowed to cut her hair without her husband's permission. Smoking in bed is illegal.

? can you have a sex change and then become a nun

Yes. Sister Mary Clark, born Michael Clark, became a nun in the small denomination American Catholic Church. Not all churches will accept transsexuals.

what country is the most sexually active in the world

Greece is the world's most sexually active country, with adults having sex 138 times per year on average. Croatia is 2nd with 134.

which is the only country in europe where you can marry someone who's already dead

According to French law, a marriage between a living person and a dead person can take place as long as it can be shown they had intended to marry.

what determines the sex of a crocodile when it hatches

The temperature at which a Nile crocodile's eggs are incubated will determine its sex. High or low produces females, intermediate produces males.

? is it true there is a product you can put on your skin before you get a tattoo to stop it hurting

There are local anaesthetics which you can rub on your skin, but they're not advised before a tattoo, as they make the skin swell, distorting the design.

? how do i cosmic order, please

What a good idea. Apparently, cosmic ordering will replace religion and unite mankind. To do it, empty your mind, then focus on what you want – politely.

? what song would be good to use for a video showing pictures of bbc casualty

AQA suggests Bonnie Tyler's 'I Need a Hero'; 'Save Me' by Jem; 'National Health' by The Kinks; 'Bad Medicine' by Bon Jovi; and 'Hospital Food' by The Eels.

? how long is the penis of the californian banana slug

> The penis of the Californian Banana Slug is approximately 100 mm long. After sexual intercourse, the Banana Slug chews off the penis of its partner.

? what is the longest kiss underwater record without oxygen

> The longest underwater kiss was 2 minutes 18 seconds, and was set in Tokyo, Japan, in April 1980. International Kissing Day is on 5 February.

? what is the earliest known use of a condom

> The oldest known depiction of a condom is a 12–15,000-year-old cave painting in France. The oldest existing condoms date from 1640: they were found in Dudley Castle.

? can crabs live in your eyebrows

Crabs, Phthirus pubis (lice), can indeed live in your eyebrows. Oral sex can lead to infestation of the eyelashes, eyebrows, face, chest hair or scalp.

? i'm 14 weeks pregnant. can u give me some info of what 2 expect going on in my body at this point and how big would the baby b now

At week 14 your baby's body systems begin to work on their own. Your baby is approx 10–11.5 cm (3.5–4 inches) and weighs approximately 1.5 ounces.

? what should i call my boyfriend's penis

Boost his ego by calling it Mr Big Boy. Over 70% of men and 64% of women have a pet name for their genitalia. Macaulay Culkin named his penis 'Floyd'.

what product has foreskin in its ingredients

TNS (Tissue Nutrient System) Recovery Complex is an anti-wrinkle cream using foreskins from circumcised babies. It costs around £70 and has a sour smell.

how many people are having sex in the world right now

Around 6 million couples in the world are having sex right now. 240 million people will have sex today: that's 4% of the entire world's population.

how many condoms get used every night in the uk

438,056 condoms are used every night in the UK. That's 160 million per year. Condoms can stretch to 90 cm long and 45 cm wide before bursting.

? how do I find out my blood group

You can find out your blood group and do something amazing by giving blood. Visit http://www.blood.co.uk or call 08457711711 for your nearest session.

? what should a guy wear with a pair of red stilettos

A guy should wear a halter-neck or empire-line silk dress which should hug the body and fall to just below the knee. Red stilettos look best with black.

? if women are so good at multi-tasking – why can't they have sex and a headache at the same time

Multi-tasking refers to the brain's ability to process information and perform simultaneous operations. A headache cannot be defined as a 'task'.

? if i want to stuff my bra which cereal is best to use

Cereal is not the best thing to use to stuff a bra. Tissues work better. If you must use cereal, AQA recommends a soft, yielding one such as Sugar Puffs.

? is it true that women have twice as many pain receptors on their bodies than men. i'm planning an s&m party and i need to know

Women do have twice as many pain receptors as men. Women have (on average) 34 nerve fibres per square cm of facial skin compared to just 17 for men.

? can you get a gay penguin

Yes. A German zoo famously had to scrap plans to separate homosexual penguin couples for breeding purposes after protests from gay rights activists.

? what is the provenance of the term 'to be rogered'

Using 'to roger' as a slang term for sex derives from the Old Norse word 'hrotger' meaning 'spear'. It was also a slang term for the penis – hence sex.

? what happens if i hit my mate with a dirty sock full of cornflakes

If you hit your mate with a dirty sock full of cornflakes you will be eternally punished by warts, rat infestations and crumbs in your bed.

? can we make a fort

You can build a fort on private land you own, subject to planning permission. However, you cannot put soldiers in there or declare war on anyone else.

? if anyone asks you who is the best lover on the planet would you please answer guy winterflood

AQA has duly noted your request to identify Guy Winterflood as the best lover on the planet, though you didn't, rather crucially, specify which planet.

? statistically, what is the best sport to channel my son's interest into for him to become a professional, and also earn lots! my son is 3 and good at all sorts

Statistically, most people become professionals in wrestling, with 22% of people turning pro. As your son is 3, football is a better (and safer) option.

who would win in a fight between your mum and my mum?

AQA's mum is not keen on fighting, but would challenge your mum to a hard-fought game of Scrabble. Your mum needs to bring a big dictionary to win.

what is the best type of biscuit to make a mattress from

The best type of biscuits to make a mattress from would be fig rolls or strawberry newtons. They would be soft but still provide some back support.

how many erections does a man have on average each day

The average man has 11 erections per day, 9 of them while asleep. On average, a man will have spent 3 years of his life with an erect penis.

? i'm ginger, give me a remedy

It's not possible to permanently
change one's hair colour. Take pride
in being ginger; it's a sign of strong
character. Less than 2% of humans
are ginger.

**? aqa you are my best friend.
nobody understands me like
you. would you like to come
to a party on saturday**

AQA is pleased to be appreciated and
thinks you are great too. Sadly, AQA
is not entirely human and cannot
come to your party. Thanks for the
invite.

**? why is it acceptable for
kermit the frog to have a
romantic relationship with
miss piggy – does this not
confuse the target audience
of children**

Kermit is painfully aware of the
unsuitability of an inter-species
relationship with Miss Piggy, so he
tries to avoid her. She, however, is
much kinkier.

? how long is the longest kiss

The world record for kissing is 42.5 hours, set in the Czech Republic. The kiss began on Valentine's Day, Wednesday 14 February 2007, and lasted until the Friday.

? what is the world's longest engagement

The world's longest engagement lasted 67 years. Octavio Guillen and Adriana Martinez were 15 when they got engaged and 82 on their wedding day.

? what three questions would aqa ask a blind date

Three questions to ask a blind date: 1) Most embarrassing moment and why?; 2) Dreams that are yet unfulfilled; 3) If money was no object, what would you do?

? what percentage of people get married in britain aged between 18 and 35

In 2005, the number of people who married aged between 18 and 35 was 297,790. This was 60.8% of the total number of marriages in that year, which was 489,420.

? is the term 'making the beast with two backs' a real one

'Making the beast with two backs' is a real term, and slang for sex. In *Othello*, Iago said, 'Your daughter and the Moor are now making the beast with two backs.'

? my mate is marrying my wife's dad's cousin's daughter. what relationship will we be

Your wife's dad's cousin's daughter is her cousin, so your mate will be her cousin-in-law. You're not related to your mate but you could also use this term.

? what is the perfect woman

The perfect woman would be beautiful, intelligent, humorous and considerate. You'd also share interests, allowing you to enjoy activities together.

? where did the idea of wedding rings come from

The oldest recorded exchange of wedding rings comes from ancient Egypt, 4,800 years ago. The ring was considered a supernatural never-ending band of love.

? my mate is about to receive a gq man of the year award for environmental achievements – if you give us a clever 2 liner for his speech we promise to mention you

Thank you – it's hard to make environmentalism seem cool. Vin Diesel would never have made it as an action star if he was called Vin Unleaded.

? why is the menopause called that if it doesn't happen to men

The 'meno-' in menopause is actually a Greek combined form meaning 'month' or 'moon'. The male form of menopause is called andropause ('andro' = 'male').

? is there a subconscious reason why men don't like shopping and flick channels

Men flick channels because it shows their control over the family. This behaviour's absent in matrilineal Venezuela. Men hate shopping because it's dull.

? what's the best way to cheer up

AQA suggests spending time with your friends. Think about the phrase 'every minute you are upset is 60 seconds of happiness you will never get back'.

celebrity q&a

stephen fry

who is stephen fry

A man trying to get through life
without hurting or being hurt.
Failing, but trying. For further
information, ask AQA.

what's the meaning of life

It has no meaning. The medieval
vision of a bird flying from the cold
darkness briefly through a loud,
warm room and then out again into
the freezing night is as good as any.

what gadget yet to be invented would you most like to see

A good mayonnaise-making device.
Liquidisers and food processors just
can't do it. I don't mind making it by
hand, but it would be so pleasing to
have an elegant device that did it.

? what's your funniest joke

> I stooped to pick a buttercup. Why
> people leave buttocks lying around,
> I've no idea.

**? was it your appearance in
spiceworld the movie that
set your career alight**

> Everything else since then has been
> anticlimax.

**? what questions would you
like answered before you die**

> What is electricity? No really, what is
> it? How can one write without
> smoking?

**? does writing come to you
easily or is it hard graft**

> The latter, I'm annoyed to say. Very
> annoyed.

? what is your favourite word

> Puszipajtas, pronounced pussy-pie-
> tosh. It's Hungarian and hard to
> translate. 'A friend you know well
> enough to embrace' sort of covers it.

do lemmings really jump off cliffs?

Animal facts and fiction

? are baby hedgehogs born with hard spikes and how do the mother hedgehogs not get stabbed during labour

Baby hedgehogs are born with very soft pliable spikes which are aligned to allow easy birth. These quickly harden to provide protection for the hoglet.

? how many dogs in the uk

There are around 6.8 million dogs in the UK. It is estimated that the dog population of the UK produces about 900 tonnes of faeces every single day.

? what country in the world has killed the most extinct animals

The IUCN documents 784 extinctions since AD 1500 (when historical scientific records began). Mauritius has lost most (44), followed by Australia (35).

? are there more cows than cars in the world

Yes, there are more cows in the world than cars: an estimated 1.4 billion cows compared to about 1 billion cars. Cows produce 20% of all methane.

? what creature in the animal kingdom has the biggest heart in relation to the size of its body

The hummingbird has the biggest heart of all, for the animal's size. In flight, it pumps at 1,000 times a minute so it can hover like a helicopter.

? what do u call a group of bears, like a murder of crows or a pack of wolves

The collective term for bears is a sleuth of bears. There are packs or routs of wolves and murders or storytellings of crows.

? what would happen to mankind if more animals had opposable thumbs

The first effect of the spread of opposable thumbs among mammals would be the desertion of cats – once they could open their own tins, they'd be off.

? what is the most disgusting fact you have on your database

AQA's most disgusting fact is that 184 people are bitten by rats in New York each year, but a whopping 1,102 New Yorkers are bitten by other New Yorkers.

? which bird can't walk or hop

There are many birds that can only hop, but the hummingbird is peculiar in that it cannot walk at all. It is also the only bird which can fly backwards.

? how many cats r there on the isle of dogs please

> Assuming 1 cat for every 6 residents, reflecting the national average, there are around 20,000 cats living on the Isle of Dogs, about 3,000 of them named Misty.

? were british bees wiped during one of the world wars by bee flu and did we replace them with foreign bees

> Not all British bees were wiped out, but great losses occurred in 1901–20. The cause may have been tracheal mites. New stock was imported from Europe.

? who would win in a fight, a camel or chewbacca

> Without question, Chewbacca would win a fight against a camel. Chewie stands 7ft 6in, fires guns and speaks Shyriiwook. Camels can only spit.

? can a turtle breath through its arse

Yes. Many species of turtle have special sacs opening off the cloaca (anal chamber) permitting the take-up of oxygen. Sea-cucumbers also 'butt-breathe'.

? how do you prevent wasps from nesting in palm trees

Wasps can be prevented from nesting in palm trees by removal of any dried leaves around the tree trunk. This is where wasps like to nest. Take good care.

? do cats have dreams when they sleep

Most mammals dream, including cats. Dreaming helps brains grow, by exciting the neurons. Newborn babies dream about 8 hours per day.

? do lemmings really jump off cliffs

Lemming suicide is fiction. The Disney-produced 1958 Oscar-winning documentary *White Wilderness* featured tame lemmings intentionally driven into a river.

? how many different types of chicken are there

There are around 70 common breeds of chicken. With a population of more than 24 billion, there are more chickens in the world than any other bird.

? do geese take it in turns at the front when flying

Yes, geese flying in a V take turns to lead, as the lack of any uplift from a bird in front makes it the hardest job. They switch about in order to rest.

are sheep more tolerant to loud noise than say cows and horses ie festival music

Sheep appear to acclimatise to noise more easily than other animals. This has been tested through their body and behavioural responses to aircraft noise.

what is the most expensive liquid in the world

The most expensive liquid on the planet is scorpion venom, used in medical research. It costs £1,038 for a 0.2 ml sample, which is £5,302,725 per litre.

how could i weigh an elephant without using weighing scales

Zoologists weigh elephants by taking measurements and using the formula (11.5 × girth)+(7.55 × length)+(12.5 × pad circumference) − 4016 = weight in kg.

what percentage of people in britain are scared of spiders

30% of people in the UK (17.96 million) have a fear of spiders. 84% of these are women. Stroking a tarantula is supposed to help curb fear eventually.

how many years is a cat year compared to a human year

A cat year is about 5 human years. Flook the Burmese cat received a telegram from the Queen in October 2006 as her 23 cat years are equivalent to over 100 human ones.

how old was the oldest goldfish

The oldest known goldfish was Goldie, owned by Pauline Evans of Devon. Goldie lived for 45 years after being won at a fairground in 1960.

how many little tuna tins would jaws fit into

The largest great white shark caught weighed 3,312 kg. A small tuna tin weighs around 185 g. Therefore Jaws would fill 17,903 of the small tins.

what creature has the most teeth

The creature with the most teeth is the snail – between 15,000 and 50,000. Elephants have the largest teeth – their tusks are actually modified incisors.

who would win in a fight between a sperm whale and a giant squid

A sperm whale would have a giant squid for breakfast – literally. Giant squid form 80% of its diet; the rest being octopus, fish, shrimp, crab and shark.

why do cockerels make a noise when the sun comes up

Cocks crow through a combination of sexual advertisement and territorial defence. They do this in the morning as a ritual to let others know who is boss.

how many ounces of insects do the 20 million strong bat population of bracken cave, texas, eat every night

It's been estimated that the 22,000,000 Mexican free-tailed bats roosting in Bracken Cave, Texas, eat 250 tons or 8,960,000 ounces of insects each night.

how much does an elephant poo in its life

An elephant would produce around 2,492,000 kg of poo in its life. On a daily basis they poo around 100 kg. For a human, the daily amount is around 250 g.

? what is the smallest bird in the world called

The world's smallest bird is the Cuban zunzun (Mellisuga helenae). Also known as a bee hummingbird, it measures 6 cm and is the weight of 4 paperclips.

? can u get blue sheep

The bharal (Pseudois nayaur) is called the Himalayan blue sheep; its coat has a slight blue sheen. Its predators include snow leopards and tawny eagles.

? how many sparrows are in the world

The total population of sparrows, the world's most numerous bird, is estimated to be 500 million birds, with 2.6–4.6 million breeding pairs in Britain.

? have scientists discovered sharks with legs

No, but epaulette sharks that walk with their fins across coral reefs are among more than 50 new species discovered recently off the coast of Indonesia.

? how do bats have babies

Baby bats (called 'pups') are born upside down and are caught by their mother's wings. They hang on to the mother's nipples using hooked milk teeth.

? what is the speed of acceleration of a chameleon's tongue

The chameleon's tongue whips out faster than the eye can follow, speeding at 26 body lengths per second. It hits the prey in about 0.03 seconds.

? is it true that there is a bird with a penis bigger than its body

Yes, the bird with a penis bigger than its body is the Argentine Blue-bill or Argentine Lake Duck (Oxyura vittata). Only 3% of bird species have a penis.

? what dog is the fastest swimmer and how fast is it

On average dogs can swim at 3.5 mph. Umbra, a world record holding labrador, swam 4 miles in 73 minutes. Portuguese water dogs are bred for ability in water.

? why do we and other animals cock our heads when we don't understand or are confused?

Humans and animals cock their heads when confused to allow better identification of sounds and images by listening and looking in a different plane.

mackenzie crook

who is mackenzie crook

The skinny bloke out of *The Office*.

what's the meaning of life

Peace on Earth, goodwill to all men.

what's your funniest joke

Why don't cannibals eat clowns?
Because they taste funny.

what's the best bargain you ever bought

A Gloriosa Rothschildii for £1.99 from
Homebase reduced from £25 because
it had finished flowering. I've had it
for three years now and it's produced
loads of flowers. Suckers.

do you prefer comedy or serious acting

I bloody love acting. It's an incredible
feeling to make people laugh but now
I've found out I can make people cry.
Don't know which I enjoy the most.

? what was your worst moment on stage

I 'had a fall' during my dramatic exit in *One Flew Over the Cuckoo's Nest*, skinned my knees and went on to take my bow with blood seeping through my trousers.

? if reincarnation is real, who or what would you come back as

Me again. I've forgotten loads of stuff.

? what do you think gareth keenan would say to ragetti from 'the pirates of the caribbean' if they met in a bar in slough

What do health and safety have to say about you sword-fighting with only one eye? Surely you have no depth perception?

which duck smoked a cigar in the 1970s?

Guide to the arts – music, plays and literature

what is a jingling johnny

A Jingling Johnny is a musical instrument that originated in Turkey. It consists of an ornamented pole from which bells and other jingling metals hang.

how did paul mccartney stop it raining at a concert

Paul McCartney hired three jets, at a cost of £28,000, to spray dry ice in the clouds above a concert at St Petersburg's Palace Square, thus preventing rain.

how long will it take if you looked at every piece of art in the louvre for 3 minutes a piece? how many pieces of artwork are in the louvre

The Louvre contains over 35,000 pieces of art, including the enigmatic *Mona Lisa*. It would take 105,000 minutes, 1,750 hours, or almost 73 days.

who has had the most hits but not a number 1 hit in the uk

Depeche Mode are the group with the most hits without ever having a Number 1. They have had 42 chart entries and never got a record beyond Number 4.

which part in a single shakespeare play has the most words to say

Prince Hamlet is by far the largest role in any Shakespeare play. Hamlet has 1,506 lines. Second is Falstaff with 1,200 lines, but his role spans two plays.

can you confirm that the ex-president of nigeria, olsegun obesanjo, is the stepdad of the lead singer from the lighthouse family

Yes, the mother of Lighthouse Family singer Tunde Baiyewu married Nigerian president Olusegun Obasanjo, following the death of Tunde's father.

? john peel forgot which band's name while presenting top of the pops

When John Peel first presented *Top Of The Pops* in 1968, he forgot the name of Amen Corner who were appearing that week. He next presented it in 1981.

? who was the oldest solo artist to have a top 40 hit

John Lee Hooker was 75 years 2 months old when 'Boom Boom' made no. 16 in the UK singles chart. This makes him the oldest solo artist with a Top 40 hit.

? how many times do god, lord and jesus appear in the king james bible

In the King James version of the Bible, the word God appears 4,472 times. Lord appears 7,964 times, while Jesus only appears 983 times.

? is there sponge bob squarepants churches in america and why

US fans of SpongeBob SquarePants have set up a 700-member church in his name to encourage 'simple things like having fun and using your imagination'.

? was the singer pete doherty ever the queen's poet

Pete Doherty was not the Queen's poet, but at 17 he won a competition and was chosen to travel with the British Council to Russia to perform his poetry.

? who was originally asked to write the lyrics to the song 'my way'

David Bowie was asked to write English lyrics for the French song 'Comme D'Habitude', which later became 'My Way'. He ended up with 'Life On Mars' instead.

since 1952 only 3 groups or artists have replaced themselves at number one – who are they

> Six artists have replaced themselves at no. 1: Ray Conniff, Norrie Paramor, The Shadows (four times), The Beatles, John Lennon, and Elvis Presley.

which novel has 50,000 words and has no 'e's

> Ernest Vincent Wright's 1939 novel *Gadsby* was 50,000 words without 'e's. 'Turkey' became 'a holiday bird'. Wright died on the day it was published.

what was the madness walk called

> The Madness walk is known as skanking. When Madness reunited at Madstock in 1992, the crowd skanking to 'One Step Beyond' hit 4.5 on the Richter scale.

? how did the ewan mcgregor movie 'trainspotting' derive its name

In the original novel, Begbie and Renton visit the disused Leith railway station to use it as a toilet, and an old drunkard asks if they are 'trainspotting'.

? what is the longest guitar solo ever recorded or performed by an artist in the 20th century, who and where

At 3.15pm on 21 June 2006 at the Potbelly Sandwich Works, Jef Sarver began a 48-hour guitar solo, which broke the previous world record of 44 hours.

? what are the 5 most depressing popular music tunes, ie tear-jerkers

Five depressing tear-jerkers: 'Tell Laura I Love Her', 'Seasons in the Sun', 'Old Shep', 'She's Out Of My Life', and 'Without You'. AQA is sobbing.

? which duck smoked a cigar in the 1970s

Dirty Duck was the feathered cigar-smoker who first appeared in the underground comic *Air Pirates Funnies* in 1971. His creator was Bobby London.

? what do gypsies use milk churns for

Olah Gypsies from Hungary use milk churns and other household instruments to create music. The album *Ando Foro* by Romano Drom samples this sound.

? can you tell me which no. 1 records did not mention the title in the song

The number 1 singles 'Unchained Melody' by the Righteous Brothers and 'Sadness, Part 1' by Enigma do not mention the title in the song.

**? if you know what jl pm gh
rs & dg rw rw nm mean
what does pq dd ma rd & hv
js eb cc ap mean**

> JL, PM, GH, RS are the initials of The
> Beatles. DG, RW, RW, NM are Pink
> Floyd. PQ, DD, MA, RD are The
> Kinks. HV, JS, EB, CC, AP are The
> Animals.

**? who was the original pretty
woman**

> The original 'Pretty Woman' was Roy
> Orbison's wife Claudette. Asked if she
> needed cash on going out, a friend
> said 'A pretty woman never needs any
> money.'

**? what name did daryl
walters write under**

> Mrs Darell Waters wrote under the
> name Enid Blyton. She is best known
> for the Famous Five and Secret Seven
> series. She died in 1968 at the age of
> 71.

how many legs in 12 days of christmas

There are 178 legs: 1 partridge, 2 doves, 3 hens, 4 colly birds, 6 geese, 7 swans, 8 maids with a cow each, 9 ladies, 10 lords, 11 pipers and 12 drummers.

can u suggest a piece of classical instrumental music to go with the novel 'the time traveler's wife'

Fauré's 'Pelléas & Mélisande' suite goes very well with *The Time Traveler's Wife*. Like the novel, it is atmospheric and depicts a bittersweet love story.

who would win in a fight between a thesaurus and a dictionary

A dictionary would beat a thesaurus in a fight. 'Zyxt' is in dictionaries, but not in thesauri, so the dictionary would always have the last word.

what year was mtv launched

MTV: Music Television launched at 12.01am on 1 August 1981, with the words 'Ladies and gentlemen, rock and roll,' spoken by Chief Operating Officer John Lack.

elvis presley once appeared in an advertisement – what was the product

Elvis Presley made a television commercial for 'Southern Maid Donuts' that ran in 1954. He sang the jingle 'You can get 'em piping hot'.

what is the most recorded song of all time

'Summertime', by George Gershwin, is the most recorded song of all time, with 13,324 versions (not 2,600 as often claimed). The Beatles' 'Yesterday' has been recorded around 3,000 times.

what was the longest song ever

'Longplayer' is the world's longest song. It is a 1,000-year-long piece of music which started to play on 1 January 2000 and will continue until 31 December 2999.

what book has the most pages

The longest book in the world, in terms of pages, is *The Yongle*, an ancient Chinese encyclopaedia. It comprises 22,937 manuscript pages.

are there any hit songs that start with the letter z

UK no. 1s beginning with the letter Z: 'Zambesi' by Lou Busch, 'Zing A Little Zong' by Bing Crosby and Jane Wyman, and 'Zorba's Dance' by Marcello Minerbi.

what's the earliest example of musical notation and from when does it date

The earliest example of musical notation is from 2000 BC Nippur (Sumeria), which was written in harmonies of thirds, and used the diatonic scale.

which famous american singer likes to be spanked before going on stage

Legendary 'You're So Vain' singer Carly Simon reportedly likes to be spanked by her orchestra to calm her nerves before going on stage.

has any magician ever accidentally killed or injured his assistant on stage?

Over 15 people have been killed whilst attempting the 'bullet catch' trick. Madame de Linsky was a magician's assistant killed in 1820 during one attempt.

who would play an instrument called a tiktiri

The tiktiri is a type of bagpipe from Hyderabad, India. It is often associated with snake charmers. It is also the name of an Egyptian oboe.

six men dry under things is an anagram of which 1980s band

Six Men Dry Under Things is an anagram of Dexy's Midnight Runners. The 1980s band reached no. 1 in the UK singles chart with 'Come On Eileen' in 1982.

who was first british woman to have a uk no. 1

Lita Roza was the first British woman to have a UK no. 1 with 'How Much is that Doggy in the Window?' It was Margaret Thatcher's favourite song.

celebrity q&a

pat jennings

who is pat jennings

A big-handed, softly spoken, Northern Ireland-born goalkeeper.

what's the meaning of life

To be happy and healthy, that's the most important thing.

what's your funniest joke

Buddhist monk walks into a pizzeria. The waiter comes up and says, 'Sir, what would you like?' The monk replies, 'Make me one with everything.'

what question would you most like aqa to answer for you

Why do I always miss the easy putts?

**how did it feel to score in
the charity shield**

I was surprised but I was delighted
too as it was on live television. In
those days, you could have played all
your matches without anyone seeing
you. So I was pleased it was on telly,
as it's nice to be able to watch it
again.

**what was your most
memorable international for
northern ireland**

I tried for the best part of my career
to qualify for the World Cup. So
learning that we'd qualified and then
beating the hosts (Spain) when we got
there were my best moments.

**would you ever consider a
career in irish politics**

Certainly not! No chance! I played all
my career right through the troubles
in Northern Ireland and despite
having been in the limelight, politics
is the one thing that I've always
steered clear of.

what is the most watched film ever?

The big and small screens – ads, actors and films

? in which film did paul newman keep his cowboy boots on when he had sex

Paul Newman played Earl Long in the 1989 movie *Blaze*, in which he had sex with his cowboy boots on in an affair with the stripper Blaze Starr.

? in the film dirty dancing does patrick swayze take his jacket off twice at the final dance by mistake

Johnny taking his jacket off twice is one of thirteen continuity goofs in *Dirty Dancing*. In another, Johnny puts his records back twice after talking to Neil.

? what was mixed with water to make the rain more visible in the 1952 film, singing in the rain

In the 1952 film *Singin' in the Rain*, the rain was actually water mixed with milk. They did this so the raindrops and puddles would show up on film.

what was the first advert broadcast on tv

The first TV advert was aired at 2.29pm on 1 July 1941. The Bulova Watch Company paid $9 to WNBT for a 10-second spot, aired before a baseball game.

what was banned on tv in 1965

Cigarette adverts were banned from UK television on 1 August 1965. Pipe tobacco and cigar adverts were allowed to continue until October 1991.

what was the first costume mr ben wore

Mr Benn's first costume was that of the Red Knight. In this episode, broadcast on 25 February 1971, he finds himself in medieval England, and helps a sad dragon.

? **who played dracula for the first time in a feature film and when**

Bela Lugosi played Dracula in the first-ever official film of the vampire, though Max Schreck played him first in the unofficial 1922 version, *Nosferatu*.

? **i'm watching the core with my house mate. there are far 2 many questions 2 ask u them all, so i was just wondering actually how many plot holes r there**

There are 27 plot holes and errors in the 2003 film *The Core*. One of them is when Josh enters the code of prime numbers, 1, 2, 3, etc. 1 isn't a prime number.

which actor/actress appeared in both only fools and horses and friends

Sir Richard Branson made cameo appearances in both *Only Fools and Horses* and *Friends*. He also appeared in *Casino Royale* (2006). He was born in July 1950.

what is the colour of the backdrop used in film sets and weather studios etc

The film backdrop technique 'bluescreen' actually uses green most often since green has a higher luminance value than blue and requires less light.

how many people did skippy the bush kangaroo save in total

In 91 episodes of *Skippy, The Bush Kangaroo*, Skippy and his human sidekick, Sonny, saved the lives of 39 people, plus a Siamese cat and a wombat.

? was the song 'monster mash' ever used in a film

'Monster Mash' was not only in a film, it also inspired a film musical. The film *Monster Mash* (1995), was in honour of the Bobby 'Boris' Picket 1962 song.

? is it true that et and poltergeist originally started out as the same film before being split into 2 separate films

Yes, in a roundabout way. Both *ET* and *Poltergeist* were inspired by different elements of an abandoned Spielberg project called 'Night Skies'.

? what is the most watched film ever

US evangelists Campus Crusade have organised thousands of showings of *Jesus* (1979). It's been seen by over 2 billion people; more than any other film.

**? what does bungle do now?
from rainbow**

John Leeson was one of four actors
who played Bungle in *Rainbow*. He's
now a continuity announcer for
Channel 4. He also voiced K9 in
Doctor Who.

**? what is lady helen guest
better known as**

The actress Jamie Lee Curtis can be
known as Baroness Haden-Guest, or
Lady Haden-Guest. Her husband,
Christopher, created the film *This Is
Spinal Tap*.

**? did robert de niro play the
lion in any wizard of oz play
or film**

When Robert De Niro was ten years
old he portrayed the Cowardly Lion in
a local production of *The Wizard of
Oz*. He has starred in over fifty films.

? **if you weigh a whale at a whaleway where do you weigh a pie**

> Dorothy Gale (aka Judy Garland) revealed where you can weigh a pie in *The Wizard Of Oz*, when she sang 'Somewhere over the rainbow, weigh a pie'.

? **why do telephone numbers in american films invariably contain the sequence 555**

> In the 1970s, US phone companies asked films and TV to use the prefix 555 to avoid confusion with real numbers. The Simpsons' phone number is 555-0113.

? **who has the world's biggest tv**

> The biggest television in the world is owned by the Japan Racing Association. The new Mitsubishi Diamond Vision HD LED display is over 8,000 square feet.

which male film star played a female in all his films

Lassie is a female character, but all nine of the dogs who portrayed her have been male. Pal, born on 20 June 1940, was the first dog to play Lassie.

who was the first puppet to win weakest link

On 10 December 2005, Basil Brush became the first puppet to win *The Weakest Link*. He donated his prize winnings to The Blue Peter 2005 Charity Appeal.

which presenter donated his cornea

Richard Whiteley, presenter of *Countdown*, donated his corneas so that somebody else could be given the gift of sight after his death in June 2005.

? **there is a technical name for in situation sound and a name for added sound like music that couldn't be from the situation. do you know what they are**

> In films, 'diegetic' music is that actually happening in the world of the film, e.g. on a radio. 'Non-diegetic' music is the score, added for effect.

? **what is the best film to use in hangman**

> *Zelig* is the best film to use in Hangman. Woody Allen's 1983 mockumentary has a short name with rare letters, and isn't so obscure as to be unfair.

? **did dickie davies ever swear on television**

> Dickie Davies never swore on TV, being a true pro. However, he is reputed to have once had a tiny bit of trouble saying 'cup soccer'. Think about it.

? what was the first record played on radio one

> The first song played on Radio 1 was Johnny Dankworth's 'Beefeaters', used by DJ Tony Blackburn as his theme tune. 'Flowers in the Rain' was the second song played.

? who sat in the rocking chair in bagpuss

> In *Bagpuss*, Madeleine the rag doll sat in a wicker chair. Professor Yaffle was the brains of the outfit however, based upon philosopher Bertrand Russell.

? how many movies have won the coveted 5 oscars for best picture, director, actor, actress and screenplay

> *It Happened One Night* (1934), *One Flew Over The Cuckoo's Nest* (1975) and *The Silence of the Lambs* (1991) are the only three movies to win 'The Big Five'.

? what model number is the tardis in doctor who

> The model of TARDIS that the Doctor has always used is an obsolete Type 40 TT capsule. TARDIS stands for 'Time And Relative Dimensions In Space'.

? what was the movie mistake in the sound of music

> Salzburg is on Austria's German border, not the Swiss border. The real Von Trapp family travelled 100 km to the Italian border, and crossed openly.

? why is (disney's) herbie (vw beetle) numbered 53

> Disney's Herbie is number 53 because this was the number on the uniform of baseball player Don Drysdale, a favourite of *Love Bug* producer Bill Walsh.

who would win in a fight between andi peters and dave benson phillips

AQA thinks Dave Benson Phillips would win. He wears dungarees and has puppet Chester to help out. Andi Peters would just make bad jokes throughout.

in charlie brown how did woodstock get his name

Charles M. Schulz, the creator of *Peanuts*, has acknowledged in several interviews that he took Woodstock's name from the iconic 1969 rock festival.

who died on christmas day 1977

The legendary comedian Charlie Chaplin died on Christmas Day 1977, aged 88. He was buried in the village of Corsier in the hills above Lake Geneva.

? is micky mouse still a virgin

Yes, judging by the Walt Disney cartoons, Mickey Mouse is still a virgin. AQA can find no evidence of him and Minnie ever consummating their relationship.

? how many episodes of neighbours have ever been made and if they were put onto dvd how many dvds would be needed

As of 9 February 2007, *Neighbours* has had 5,145 episodes made. It was first aired on 18 March 1985. You would need 858 DVDs to fit every *Neighbours* episode.

? susan morrisey became the first soap character to do what

In February 1999 Susannah Morrisey (*Brookside*) was the first mother to breastfeed her baby in a soap opera. The scene used a real-life mother and baby.

❓ how come they play the national anthem on bbc radio 4 just before 1am

> It was always tradition to play it at the end of transmission every night. BBC1 stopped playing it in December 1997. BBC2 and ITV stopped in the early 1990s.

❓ who does fred flintstone work for

> Fred Flintstone works for the Slate Rock & Gravel Company as a Bronto Crane Operator. It used to be called Rockhead & Quarry Cave Construction Company.

❓ 'so, let's drink to dublin' is a quote by which character and film

> 'Let's drink to Dublin' is a quote from the 1989 film *My Left Foot* (dir. Jim Sheridan). It was said by Christy Brown, who was played by Daniel Day Lewis.

what football team does postman pat support

Postman Pat supports Pencaster United. The postman's surname is Clifton and he is married to Sara. They own a black and white cat called Jess.

how much did gone with the wind gross

Gone With The Wind has grossed £196,290,339. It has sold more tickets than any film in history. The makers bought the rights to the book for £25,000.

who would win a fight against et and mr t

ET would beat Mr T. Mr T would lean over to land one on ET and the weight of his jewels would tip him over. ET would then burn his eyes out with his finger.

how much did sean connery's dinner jacket that he wore for the film thunderball go for at charity auction

Sean Connery's dinner jacket worn in *Thunderball* in 1965 was sold at auction in March 2007 for £33,600. It was made of black wool and lined with satin.

in the hanna barbera cartoon top cat, what was officer dibble's first name

Charlie was the first name of Officer Dibble in *Top Cat*. Fancy Fancy, Spook, Benny the Ball, The Brain and Choo Choo were other characters.

who would win a fight between spiderman and batman

AQA believes that Spiderman would win the fight between himself and Batman. Spiderman's real superpowers are far superior to Batman's expensive gadgetry.

? what were the cinema certifications before the introduction of 12, 15, 18

Between 1970 and 1982 UK cinema certifications were U, A, AA and X. In November 1982 U, PG, 15, 18 and Restricted 18 were introduced. 12 appeared on 1 August 1989.

? did a tv presenter once shoot herself in the head live on tv

On 15 July 1974, news presenter Christine Chubbuck read out three news reports for Suncoast Digest, then produced a gun and shot herself dead, live.

? what's the name of the homeless fashion movement in zoolander

The fashion range inspired by homeless people in the film *Zoolander* is called Derelicte. Blue Steel is Zoolander's famous look. Magnum is his new one.

who invented the pub?

Gastronomy – a connoisseur's guide to food and drink

? what is the name given to the largest sized beer barrel

The largest sized barrel of beer is called a tun, and contains 216 gallons, or 1,728 pints. A firkin is the smallest, containing 9 gallons, or 72 pints.

? how many eggs does the average human eat in their life

The average human eats 13,840 eggs in their lifetime. There are also 10.426 billion eggs eaten in the UK per year, from 28.7 million laying hens.

? which fish caught in britain do you have to offer to the queen

Sturgeon caught in Britain must be offered to the Queen under a law that dates back to the 14th century. The same law applies to dolphin and porpoise.

? how many eggs would you need to make a pancake the size of the o2 dome base

To make a pancake the size of the O2 dome's base, you would need 6,661,250 eggs, 366.37 tonnes of flour, 999,187.5 litres of milk and a huge pan.

? how many beers are consumed every second in the uk

The number of pints of beer consumed every second in the UK is 324.07. 28 million pints of beer are drunk every day. There are 86,400 seconds in a day.

? which meal will british people eat more than 3000 times in a lifetime

Government research has found that the average British person eats 3,000 meals of spaghetti bolognese in their lifetime. Stew is second (2,612 meals).

❓ which country eats hamsters

Hamsters have long been revered in Peru and other South American countries as a culinary delicacy. Their meat is fairly low in calories and succulent.

❓ what is a glissgliss

The edible dormouse or fat dormouse (Glis glis) is a small dormouse and the only species in the genus Glis. It was farmed and eaten by the ancient Romans.

❓ what are love apples

Love apples are tomatoes. In the 16th century tomatoes were known in Italy as pomo dei Mori; transliterated to the French pomme d'amour, 'love apple'.

❓ is a peanut a pea or a nut

A peanut is neither a pea nor a nut. In fact, both peanuts and peas are legumes. Legumes are the fruits or seeds of anything that comes in a pod.

? why does english coca cola taste different to foreign coca cola

Coca Cola taste varies as the Coca Cola Co makes a syrup which bottlers mix with water and sweeteners. More or less sweetener is used in different places.

? give me 3 statistics that will wow my friends

Facts: 76 people die each year playing Twister; Linda McCartney sold more veggy meals than Paul sold records; humans share 1/3 of their DNA with lettuce.

? is it true that the treaty of versailles that ended world war 1 also stated that sparkling wine could be called champagne only if it came from that region

The 1891 Treaty of Madrid stated only wine produced in the Champagne region could be called champagne. This was reaffirmed in the Treaty of Versailles.

where did mince pies come from

The origins of the mince pie are in the medieval pastry, chewette, which contained liver or chopped meat (mince) mixed with boiled eggs and ginger.

what are glass noodles made from

Glass noodles are gossamer, translucent threads that are not really noodles in the traditional sense, but are made from the starch of green mung beans.

is walnut an ingredient of dynamite

It is peanuts that can be used in dynamite. Peanut oil can also be used in making glycerol, which in turn is used to make the explosive nitroglycerine.

? have men ever appeared on the good housekeeping cover

Jamie Oliver became the first man in 70 years to grace the cover of *Good Housekeeping* magazine. The previous cover-man was King George VI in 1937.

? why do triangle sandwiches taste better than rectangle ones

72% of Britons prefer triangular sandwiches. They taste better because they encourage a small bite, releasing flavour molecules more effectively.

? what is the most expensive flavour jam

The world's most expensive jam is a redcurrant jam from a 14th-century recipe made in the tiny French town of Bar-le-Duc.

? what are the seven ways to cook an egg

The seven ways to cook an egg are: boil it, fry it, poach it, scramble it, coddle it, bake it and make it into a plain omelette. AQA prefers scrambled egg.

? does the queen have crusts on cucumber sandwiches at garden parties

At a Buckingham Palace Garden Party, there are no crusts on cucumber, smoked salmon or asparagus sandwiches. The garden parties cost £500,000 per year.

? how big is the world's largest teabag

The world's biggest ever teabag was 4 metres by 3 metres, and made 11,000 cups of Earl Grey. It was made in 2003 to celebrate Twinings' 300th birthday.

? what is special about the way spaghetti snaps

It is impossible to snap dry spaghetti into two pieces. The shock of the initial break sends a wave along the strand of pasta, causing more breaks.

? is an aubergine a fruit

An aubergine is a fruit (technically a berry), as it grows on a plant and contains seeds. It is, however, treated as a vegetable in savoury dishes.

? how many different wines are there in the world

At any given moment, there are over 60,000 different wines commercially available in the world. Wine has been made for at least 7,000 years.

? does nutmeg get you high

When eaten in excess (more than a teaspoon), nutmeg can cause hallucinations, nausea, stomach pains and severe fatigue. It is not recommended.

what is the best parmesan cheese

Parmigiano Reggiano Stravecchio is considered the best Parmesan cheese, as it is aged for three years. Parmesan is the most shoplifted product in Italy.

why does cream go stiff when whipped

Cream goes thick when whipped because you are mixing it with air. It doubles the cream's volume, capturing air bubbles in a network of fat droplets.

random, but what was that fact about fish parts (gall bladders) being used to purify beer

Isinglass is derived from the swim-bladders of certain fish from tropical waters. It's added to beer to remove haze and leave it clear, aiding filtration.

❓ name the champagne bottle sizes

Champagne bottle sizes: bottle (0.75l); magnum (1.5l); jeroboam (3l); rehoboam (4.5l); methuselah (6l); salmanazar (9l); balthazar (12l); nebuchadnezzar (15l).

❓ when were crisps invented

The first crisps were invented by Native American/African-American chef George Crum, at Moon's Lake House near Saratoga Springs, New York, in August 1853.

❓ how many oranges would need to be placed end to end to make it to the moon

The Earth is 238,900 miles from the moon. You would need 13,411 oranges to cover a mile, so to the moon you would need 3,203,935,680 oranges end to end.

how many varieties in heinz

Henry Heinz adopted the slogan '57 Varieties' because he liked the numbers 5 and 7. Including divisions and subsidiaries, they actually have around 1,300.

what is the most expensive dessert

Grand Opulence is a sundae available at New York's Serendipity restaurant for a mere $1,000. Edible gold leaf and caviar are ingredients.

why does alcohol make you drunk

Alcohol makes you drunk because it slows the function of the brain and increases the release of the neurotransmitter dopamine, which is related to pleasure.

what is the name of the bumps on a raspberry

The 'bumps' are called drupelets. The raspberry is not a berry at all, but an aggregate fruit of numerous drupelets around a central core.

how many pringles are eaten in britain every year

About 150 million tubes of Pringles are sold in the UK every year, weighing 25,500 tonnes. At 95 crisps per can, that's 14.25 billion Pringles.

what is the world record for the largest picnic and where was it held

The record for the world's largest picnic was broken on Sunday 3 August 2003, when 1,325 people gathered in Manhattan's Bryant Park. Everyone brought food.

u will go through 121 pints of this in your life – what is it

It is said that we will go through 121 pints of tears in our lifetime. The average person will also eat 10,000 chocolate bars and have 7,163 baths.

? what's the best restaurant in peru to eat guinea pigs

> The Inka Grill, on the Plaza De Armas, Cusco, Peru, serves delicious cuy (guinea pig). They used to serve alpaca meat, before it was made illegal.

? when, where and by whom were bourbon biscuits invented

> The Bourbon biscuit was introduced in 1910 by the Peek Frean biscuit company in Bermondsey. They also introduced the Garibaldi.

? why does cheese melt

> Most cheeses melt between 55°C and 82°C. When enough protein bonds are broken within the cheese from the heat, it will turn from a solid to a viscous liquid.

how many rice krispies are there in your average bowl of cereal

In the average 30g bowl of Kellogg's Rice Krispies there will be around 2,000 individual cooked grains of rice. Rice Krispies have been around since 1928.

what's the average price of a pint of beer in the world

Average price of a pint of beer in the world: £2.12, US$4.22, 3.12 euros, 513.79 Japanese yen, 520.22 Spanish pesetas, or 0.00628970 gold ounces.

who invented the pub

The Romans invented the pub. It was established when the Roman road network was being built so that the weary traveller could obtain refreshment.

? how much money has the man who invented coke earned

> Doctor John Pemberton, the man who invented Coca Cola in 1896, sold the formula for the drink for just $2,300 in 1897.

? what is the patron saint of breweries

> Saint Arnulf of Metz was born to a prominent Austrian family in AD 580 and is the patron saint of beer and breweries. He said beer was better than water to drink.

? give me a list with every country in the world that doesn't have mcdonald's fast food

> There are no McDonald's outlets in Greenland, Mongolia, Kazakhstan, most of the Middle East, Guyana, Papua New Guinea, Burma, Vietnam and most of Africa.

ronnie o'sullivan

? **who is ronnie o'sullivan**

> I'm a dad, a snooker player and a nice
> guy.

? **you said in an interview**
early in your career that
you hated losing. do you
still feel that way

> It still really hurts at times – but you
> know that being a sportsman it's
> bound to happen now and then.

? **how much satisfaction did it**
give you whitewashing
former world champion
runner-up rex williams
when playing him left
handed instead of your
normal right handed

> Who? Did I? Just the same as
> whitewashing anyone else.

? if you could swap being the
best snooker player in the
world for one thing, what
would it be

> The best snooker player of all time.

? are you obsessed with
snooker

> Not really. I used to be. Now I like
> doing it well. But it isn't everything
> to me.

? you are regarded by many
as a sex symbol. does this
fill you with pride or do you
not care one little bit

> I don't really care. The only thing I
> might care about it is who's saying it!

do banana trees walk?

Lessons in history, geography and the wider world

which is the world's only car-free city centre

Groningen in The Netherlands is the world's only car-free city, with bikes the main form of transport.
Congestion led city planners to dig up the roads.

what is the most common place name in the world

The most common place name in the world is San Jose, of which there are 1,716. They're named after San Jose (Saint Joseph), the patron saint of workers.

which country has the second-largest road network

India has the second largest road network in the world, with over 3 million km of roads, of which 46% are paved. 40 million vehicles use the roads.

? what was introduced in 1567, abolished in 1826 and re-introduced in 1994

> Queen Elizabeth I held the first national lottery in 1567. Lotteries were banned in 1826 and returned in 1994. A lottery paid for Westminster Bridge in 1730.

? which country in africa has never been colonised

> Ethiopia is the one African country which was never colonised by the European empires, though Italy conquered it in 1936, eventually withdrawing in 1941.

? what's the longest-standing record in the guinness book of records

> The *Guinness Book of Records* longest-standing record is held by St Simeon the Stylite (circa AD 386–459), who spent 29 years sitting on a stone pillar.

? if orleans in america is new orleans, where is the original orleans

> The original Orléans is in France, and is known as the capital of the Loire Valley region. The sanctified Joan of Arc was known as the 'Maid of Orléans'.

? after neil armstrong said that's one small step for man one giant leap for mankind, what were his next few lines

> After his 'One Small Step' speech, Armstrong continued: 'Yes, the surface is fine and powdery. I can kick it up loosely with my toe.'

? to the nearest metre, how far underwater is the world's deepest post box

> The world's deepest post box is located 10 metres beneath the waters of Susami Bay, Japan. It is used by divers and emptied daily by the post office.

do banana trees walk

Banana plants can move up to 15 cm per year. This is because they have no central root, but lateral roots which grow and move towards the sun.

can u give me the most amazing, crazy, outrageous yet plausible fact to wow people with this evening please

In 1386, a pig in France was executed by public hanging for the murder of a child. Earth is the only planet not named after a god. Slugs have four noses.

what's the nearest commonwealth country to the uk

The nearest Commonwealth country to the UK is Malta. There are 53 countries in total in the Commonwealth. Canada is the largest and Australia the second largest.

? which town or city in the uk has the highest life expectancy and what is that age

London borough Kensington & Chelsea, at 80.8 (men) & 85.8 (women) years, has the highest life expectancy. Glasgow, at 69.3 & 76.4 years, has the lowest.

? what is 28 august bank holiday in aid of

In 1871 John Lubbock designated the first Monday in August a bank holiday due to cricket. In 1971 the last Monday was added to extend the tourist season.

? in which town do they make cat's eyes

Cat's eyes (trademark Catseye) are manufactured in Halifax. Inventor Percy Shaw was born there and developed them in 1933, when tram lines were removed.

？ what is the world record for hula hooping

The hula hooping world record is 90 hours, set by American Roxanne Rose in 1987. Australian Kareena Oates twirled 100 hoops simultaneously in 2005.

？ which country in the world has the longest name

With 63 letters, Al Jumahiriyah al Arabiyah al Libiyah ash Shabiyah al Ishtirakiyah al Uzma, also known as Libya, is the longest country name in the world.

？ do mice squeak

House mice squeak to each other in their nest. It was recently discovered that males produce ultrasonic songs in response to female sex pheromones.

what is the world's oldest tree

At over 4,800 years old, the oldest living tree is 'Methuselah', a bristlecone pine in the White Mountains, California. Its exact location is a secret.

what did queen victoria ban from her funeral

Queen Victoria banned the colour black from her funeral, instructing mourners to wear white. Even the weather obliged – the ground was covered with snow.

how many countries in the world end in the word land and what are they

Twelve countries end in 'land': England, Finland, Greenland, Iceland, Ireland, New Zealand, N. Ireland, Poland, Swaziland, Scotland, Switzerland and Thailand.

second man in space

Alan Shepard (1923–98) was the second man, and the first US astronaut, in space in May 1961. Prior to launch he said, 'Please, dear God, don't let me fuck up.'

distil the 21st century into 21 words

Youtube, iPod, mobile phones, reality TV, celebrity, obesity, cheap flights, global warming, tsunami, oil, intolerance, Bush, Blair, Osama, Iraq, suicide bombers.

how many languages are spoken in london

Within the boundaries of the capital, 300 different languages are regularly spoken. This makes London the most cosmopolitan city in the world.

? what nationality was the first pilot to be saved by an ejector seat

German test pilot Helmut Schenk was the first to be saved by an ejector seat. He escaped from an iced-up Heinkel He-280 jet fighter on 13 January 1942.

? which is highest, the millennium wheel or the new wembley stadium arch

The Wembley Stadium arch is higher than the Millennium Wheel. The arch is 133 m high, but reaches 140 m above the ground, 5 m higher than the wheel.

? how deep is the deepest point of ocean on earth & how far down can the best submarines go

The deepest point is 10,924 m below sea level in Mariana Trench, Pacific Ocean. The US Navy bathyscaphe *Trieste* reached the bottom in 1960.

? who was the last known person to be hung, drawn and quartered in england

Scottish spy David Tyrie was the last person to be hanged, drawn and quartered in England, in Portsmouth on 24 August 1782 for 'treasonable correspondence'.

? who invented toilet roll

Joseph Gayetty invented flat toilet paper in 1857. Toilet roll was invented in 1867 by Thomas, Edward and Clarence Scott, who established the Scott Paper Co.

? how much money is made a day in the bank of england mint

The Bank of England produces £26,731,450 per day in banknotes. The Royal Mint is responsible for producing coins and issues 4.1 million new coins per day.

? how many space shuttle missions have there been

As of July 2007, there have been 118 space shuttle missions, with a total of 1,109 days in flight. There are a further three missions planned for 2007.

? when and where was the first ever car crash

French engineer Nicolas-Joseph Cugnot developed the steam car. In 1771, he had the first car crash when his vehicle hit a wall at the Paris Arsenal.

? 8 women have only ever appeared in what

Only eight women have ever appeared on the FBI's 'Ten Most Wanted' fugitives list. As of May 2007, 486 people had appeared on the list and 455 were located.

? what was the name of the roman emperor who charged the people tax on their urine

The urine tax was levied by Emperor Nero for the collection of urine. His successor, Vespasian, re-introduced the tax and applied it to all public toilets.

? which us state has more caribou than people

Alaska, with its more than 30 herds, has nearly double the number of caribou (around 1,000,000) than people (around 500,000).

? where is the centre of england

A 2002 survey by the Ordnance Survey pinpointed Lindley Hall Farm, near Fenny Drayton, Leics, as England's centre. Historically, Meriden claimed this title.

? what time is it in the poles

> Time zones divide along lines of
> longitude and meet at the poles,
> causing them to be in all time zones.
> The South Pole is on the same time as
> New Zealand.

**? what is the biggest car park
in the world**

> West Edmonton Mall in Edmonton,
> Alberta, Canada, has the world's
> largest car park, with space for over
> 20,000 vehicles. Others say it's the
> M25.

**? what is the only city in the
uk which is made up of the
first half of the alphabet**

> Lichfield is the only UK city whose
> letters are all in the first half of the
> alphabet. It has a population of just
> 28,000, and is famous for its
> cathedral.

what are the 5 countries that when spelt in capital letters, none of the letters can be coloured in

Countries that contain no enclosed letters when written in capitals include: CHILE, FIJI, LIECHTENSTEIN, NIGER, NIUE, SEYCHELLES and YEMEN.

what's the highest elevated airfield in the world

The world's highest airfield is San Rafael airport in Peru, at 14,422 feet. The highest commercial airfield is Qamdo Bangda airport in Tibet (14,219 ft).

what top 5 inventions come from canada

Canadians voted the top five Canadian inventions as: insulin (1921), the phone (1876), the light bulb (1874), 5-pin bowling (1908) and the Wonderbra (1964).

what's the longest town in ireland

Muckanaghederdauhaulia in Galway (22 letters) is the longest town name in Ireland and means pig-marsh between two seas. It's the world's longest port name.

if bees die out what will we lose

If bees die out, everything will die within an estimated four years. Most food crops rely on bees to pollinate them, so if bees die out, so do humans.

1st ever female british doctor

Elizabeth Garrett Anderson was the UK's first female doctor, gaining membership of the BMA in 1873. In 1908, she became England's first female mayor.

? who made the first ever mobile phone call

Motorola's Martin Cooper made the first mobile call to his Bell Laboratories rival Joel Engel on 3 April 1973. The UK's first was by Ernie Wise on 1 January 1985.

? what is the smallest island the population of the world could stand on

The world's population requires some 1,054 sq km, so Cameron Island, a desolate Arctic island off Canada, could just squeeze them on to its 1,059 sq km.

? what is the oldest armed force

The Swiss Guard is the world's oldest army. The earliest detachment was in 1497 and the Papal Swiss Guard in the Vatican (est. 1506) still exists today.

which underground station had the first moving staircase installed

Earl's Court was the first tube station to install escalators on 4 October 1911. One-legged 'Bumper' Harris rode them to assure passengers of their safety.

what's the oldest living plant species

King's Lomatia of Tasmania is the oldest living plant species. Its fossils date back 43,600 years. As it's sterile, it clones itself when a branch falls.

what is the oldest film footage of a battle

The Battle of Paardeberg (18–27 February 1900) in the Boer War is believed to be the oldest film footage of war. It was shown in *We Stand On Guard* (2001).

top 5 populated cities in the world

The five most populous cities in the world are Mumbai in India (13.1 million), Karachi in Pakistan (11.6 million), Delhi (11.5 million), Sao Paulo (11 million) and Moscow (10.7 million).

how many us flags have been left on the moon

Six US flags were placed on the moon – one for each of Apollo 11, 12, 14, 15, 16 and 17. However, the force of the engine on ascent may have knocked some over.

how many human blood cells would it take to fill an olympic sized swimming pool

It would take 147.5 million trillion human blood cells to fill an Olympic-sized swimming pool. An Olympic swimming pool holds 2.5 million litres.

? who was the president of france in 1946

France had no presidents in 1946. However, it did have four 'chairmen of the provisional government'. They were de Gaulle, Gouin, Bidault and Blum.

? what were the last words spoken on the moon

Last words on the moon: 'We leave as we came and, God willing, as we shall return, with peace and hope for all mankind. Godspeed the crew of Apollo 17.'

? i once saw a coin that could be broken into quarters with each piece representing a quarter of the whole coin's value – what is the coin called as no one believes me

Spanish dollars were silver coins that were sometimes cut into four or eight pieces. From this, the terms 'two bits', 'quarter' and 'pieces of eight' are derived.

how much money will the average person in the uk spend in their lifetime?

Work, play and shopping

? **a person pushes a car to a hotel. when they get there the person gives the hotel owner some money, what for**

They are both taking part in a game of Monopoly – the person using the car counter has landed on the square belonging to the other player, so pays rent.

? **who are the top 3 biggest employers in the world in terms of staff**

The top three employers worldwide are Walmart (2.4 million people), the Chinese Army (2.3 million) and the Indian State Railways (1.5 million). The NHS is fourth.

? **who invented the twistable lipstick dispenser**

American James Bruce Mason Jr patented the first swivel lipstick tube in 1923. The first tubes of lipstick were made by Maurice Levy of Connecticut in 1915.

who was born in 1959 and couldn't bend her legs until 1965, mostly associated with horses, has a brother called todd and two sisters

Barbie, the famous doll, was 'born' in 1959, couldn't bend her legs until 1965, and has a brother called Todd. She used to have two sisters, but now has five.

where might I get enough beer towels to make a suit out of

Beer towels can be purchased from bargizmos.co.uk (01952 618877). You can choose from a range of logos. AQA estimates you will need around 65 for a suit.

in 2005 how many vacuum cleaners were sold in the uk

Over 6 million (6,002,000) vacuum cleaners were sold in the UK in 2005. 52% were cylinder models and 44% upright; other types accounted for the rest.

? if a person in their 80s is an octogenarian, what are people in their 30s and 40s

Someone in their 30s is a tricenarian and someone in their 40s is a quadragenarian. Someone over 100 is a centenarian and over 110 is a supercentenarian.

? how much money will the average person in the uk spend in their entire lifetime

On average, UK men will spend £1,717,118 in their lifetime. Of that, £286,311 goes to the taxman. Women spend somewhat less; just £1,363,729.

? who designed german ss uniforms

The all-black German SS uniform was designed by Hugo Boss in 1932. It is considered one of the most recognisable military uniforms in history.

? is it possible to make your own hair gel/wax

To make your own hair gel, mix 1 teaspoon of unflavoured gelatine with 1 cup of warm water. Keep it refrigerated. This gel isn't suitable for vegetarians.

? how much would it cost to hypothetically buy every single property in england

There are approximately 21 million households in England. The average house price is £195,000. To buy them all would cost you roughly £4.1 trillion.

? what tubes resulted in 73 accidents in britain in 2002

Toothpaste tubes cause 73 accidents per year. Surprisingly, 823 accidents are caused by letters and envelopes. Take care opening your post tomorrow.

? do the guys that paint the lines on the road get paid more than firefighters

A survey carried out in 2006 found that white line painters are earning £53,000 per annum, compared to a fire-fighter's average salary of £25,000.

? try to scare me

One person every 10 minutes dies from cardiovascular disease. You are never more than a few feet from a rat in London. Most lipstick contains fish scales.

? how many deaths and injuries have been caused by safety pins

An average of 150 people are injured every year by safety pins. In 2002, 738 people were injured by zips, and in 2001, 839 were injured by paperclips.

? what percentage of prisoners in the uk are mothers

Around 80% of female prisoners in the UK are mothers. A third have children under five. Their children are 5–6 times more likely to be imprisoned in the future.

? how many miles does the average woman walk whilst hoovering during an average lifetime

An average woman walks 7,300 miles in her lifetime whilst vacuuming. Men only walk an average of 850 miles. They ought to make it up by doing the dishes.

? is there anything in the average household that would act as an antibiotic

Garlic is a natural antibiotic, found in the average house, which kills infecting bacteria and protects the body from bacterial poisons. Another is honey.

? what is the man called on the monopoly board

Rich Uncle Pennybags is the rotund old man in a top hat who serves as the mascot of the game Monopoly. He is modelled after John Davison Rockefeller.

? how many cigarettes get smoked a year in england

More than 70 billion cigarettes are smoked in the UK every year. AQA estimates 58.5 billion of those are smoked in England. 24% of UK adults are smokers.

? what make of dog was it in as good as it gets and how much do they cost

Verdell, the dog in the 1997 movie *As Good as It Gets*, was played by various Brussels Griffons. Puppies start from £400, and adults weigh 3.6–4.5 kg.

? what electronic item stocked by currys since 1963 have they just stopped selling

Currys have stopped selling audio cassette tapes following a drop in sales. They only sold 100,000 last year, but in 1989 they sold 83 million tapes.

? how was lip gloss invented

Lip gloss was invented by Max Factor in 1928 to make film actors' lips shiny. Ingredients are castor oil, beeswax and flavouring.

? you could burn 25 extra calories a day by wearing what

Wearing jeans can help burn 25 calories a day. A survey discovered that dressing casually leads to burning off enough calories to lose two pounds a year.

? what does h & m stand for

H&M stands for Hennes & Mauritz. Mauritz Widforss was the name of the shop that became its original premises, while 'Hennes' is Swedish for 'hers.'

? which herb best repels blackfly

Chives are said to benefit soft fruits and carrots. They can repel blackfly and greenfly and are said to help roses recover from blackspot and also improve scent.

? when was la mer made originally

La Mer moisturiser was originally developed by Max Huber in about 1957 after about 6,000 experiments and a lab explosion which hit him in the face.

celebrity q&a

danny wallace

? who is danny wallace

I'm a journalist, producer and comedian who writes about and makes programmes of a rather silly nature. I also live in the East End, and have at least one scar to prove it.

? what's the meaning of life

Be nice, get involved, have fun.

? what's your funniest joke

What's 'ET' short for? He's got little legs.

? what's the best bargain you ever bought

A kitten for a penny.

? did you dream last night – what was it about

Yes. I was running through gardens shouting a lot. I seemed fairly happy about it.

? you started your own micronation called lovely and submitted an entry for the eurovision song contest. How upset were you when you were not allowed to enter

Very upset. The song was an immaculate work of brilliance, entitled 'Stop the Mugging, Start the Hugging'. It would possibly have solved all world problems.

? did working with anne robinson on test the nation send shivers up your spine or is she really a pussycat

She's very nice to me. But then I do bow a lot.

? what three luxury items would you wish to have with you if you were cast away on a desert island

A curryhouse, a butler, and a pub.

how many sheets of a4 would all the world's trees make?

A degree of maths, medicine and science

if a gnat bit the skin of a hiv positive heroin addict and then bit you straight after, would you get the disease

Scientific studies have shown that insects cannot transfer HIV (even in heavily infected nations), as the insect injects saliva, not the previous blood.

what is the second most commonly used letter in the english language

The most commonly used letters in the English Language, based on their use in the *Oxford English Dictionary*, are, in descending order, EARIOTNSLCUDP MHGBFYWKVXZJQ.

how many sheets of a4 would be made if all the world's trees were cut down

If all 170 billion of the world's trees were cut down and used to make paper, there would be 215,000,000,000,000,000 (215 quadrillion) sheets of A4.

how many combinations of coins are there to make 50p

There are 449 ways to make 50p from combinations of 50p, 20p, 10p, 5p, 2p and 1p coins. There are 4,563 ways to make £1 (including the £1 coin).

how old is the moon

The moon is around 4.5 billion years old. It was formed by a collision between the Earth and a very large object. It is about 384,400 km from the Earth.

what are the four main blood groups

The four blood groups are O, A, B and AB. O is most common (45% of the UK population). AB is rarest, at 3%. All UK people were O before the Vikings invaded.

how many pints would it take to fill the thames

The River Thames is 346 km long, with an average width of 32 m, and an average depth of 7.01 m, so you would need 136,556,608,961 pints.

where is the smallest muscle in the human body

The smallest muscle in the human body is the stampedes. It is located in the middle ear, and is a mere 1.27 mm in length. It controls the stirrup bone.

which is the most abundant element in the human body by mass

The most abundant element in the human body is oxygen. It makes up 43 kg of mass per 70 kg of body weight. The least abundant is tungsten.

how can maggots be used 2 deduce the age of a corpse

Blowflies are rapidly attracted to the odours of decaying tissue. By ageing the adults and larvae on a corpse, a coroner can establish the time of death.

? **why does a swarm of midges not get knocked to the ground when it's raining**

A falling raindrop creates a tiny pressure wave ahead (below the raindrop). This wave pushes the midge sideways and the drop misses it.

? **what is an itch**

An itch is a sensation felt on the skin that causes a person to desire to scratch. Itches are often caused by dirt becoming trapped in pores and follicles.

? **why do magic candles never go out when you blow them**

Trick candles usually have magnesium flakes added to the wick that is capable of being ignited by the relatively low temperature of the hot wick ember.

? can tears come out of nostrils

> Yes. The nasolacrimal duct at the corner of the eye connects to the nasal cavity, draining excess tears, so we need to blow our nose when we cry.

? what is the name of the part of the leg behind the knee

> The space at the back of the human knee-joint is called the popliteal fossa. It houses the popliteal artery and six or seven popliteal lymph glands.

? why above a certain speed does it appear that rotarblades reverse their direction

> Due to the eye's sampling frequency, a blade travelling 350 degrees clockwise between optical snapshots tricks us into perceiving this as 10 degrees anticlockwise.

how many cigarettes were smoked in the world today

15 billion cigarettes were smoked worldwide today. China grows 39% of the world's tobacco. Three cigarettes contain enough nicotine to kill you.

what colour is a red bus

The London Bus colour red is S1085-Y80R (using NCS for paint); M:100, Y:91 (using CMYK). There is no Pantone reference, but the closest is Pantone 485C.

how does paracetamol know where to go to the seat of the pain

Paracetamol blocks the production of prostaglandins involved in pain transmission. Unlike ibuprofen, it blocks them in the brain, not at the pain source.

i'm 21 and male, what is the fastest muscle in my body

> Your eye muscle is the fastest muscle in your body. It can contract in under 1/100th of a second. This is the same for a human of any sex or age.

dear aqa, what is the oldest dated photograph and what is it of, please

> The oldest photograph was taken in 1826 by Frenchman Joseph Nicephore Niepce. It is titled 'View from the window at le Gras'. The exposure took eight hours.

what substance was measured in gillettes after razor blades were fired into it

> The strength of early lasers was unofficially measured in Gillettes, named after the power needed to burn a hole in one razor blade.

how heavy are all the human organs

The liver is the heaviest internal organ, weighing on average 2 kilos. The heart weighs 350 grams, the brain 1.25 kilos, and kidneys are 150 grams each. The skin weighs 4–5 kilos.

how many nuclear weapons are there on the earth

There are approximately 30,000 nuclear weapons in the world, belonging to nine countries. More than 1,500 of them are ready to launch at a moment's notice.

what was the first monkey in space

Albert II became the first monkey in space on 14 June 1949. The first monkey astronaut was Albert I, but his mission failed. Both monkeys died.

? where is the biggest diamond in the galaxy

The huge cosmic gem BPM 37093 (aka Lucy) has been estimated at 10 decillion carats (1 then 34 zeros). It can be found in the constellation of Centaurus.

? if dublin was to double in size every day, how many days would it take until it covered the whole world

Dublin is 115 square kilometres. The surface area of the world is 510,065,600 square kilometres. If it doubled in size each day, it would take 23 days.

? how many sphincters do people have

A sphincter is a circular muscle which maintains constriction of a natural body passage. There are at least 40 different sphincters in the human body.

? how much room would 5 million pounds in two pence pieces take up and how much would it weigh

£5 million is equal to 250 million 2 pence coins. These coins would have a volume of 267.38 cubic metres, and would weigh 1,780 tonnes.

? how many atoms makes up a beer mat

There are 26 quintillion atoms in a grain of sand, so AQA estimates a beer mat contains 520 sextillion atoms – more if it's topped with spillage.

? what is s(ch2ch2c1)2

$S(CH_2CH_2Cl)_2$ is more commonly known as mustard gas. It has a molecular weight of 159.08 and its chemical name is Bis(2-chloroethyl) sulphide.

? what happens when you put slices of cucumber on your eyes

Cucumber acts as a mild astringent, ie it shrinks or constricts body tissue. As a result, it can reduce puffiness of the eyes in the short term.

? i have 122 tonnes of something. can you give me the equivalent in ten different items such as animals and buses and other strange items

122 tonnes is 134,066 ducks, 16.2 double-decker buses, 4,303,423 human eyeballs, 1,742,857 mobile phones, 110,909,091 Smarties, or 34,269,662 pennies.

? if everyone on earth jumped
in the sea at the same time
and urinated would the sea
level rise and would it
change the acidity of the
sea? by how much

> Everyone urinating in the sea would
> add 1,800,000 cubic metres of liquid,
> raising the water level
> 0.000000498440435 cm. Change in
> acidity would be infinitesimal.

? can you tell me how many
babies you can fit end to end
in a blue whale's artery?
answers on a postcard

> Answers don't need to be on a
> postcard when they can be on a
> phone. You'd need 11,580,000,000
> babies to fit end to end in a blue
> whale's arterial system.

? how many colours are there

There are infinitely many wavelengths between 380 and 740 nanometres – the visible spectrum of light. This means there is an infinite number of colours.

? do all plants flower

Not all plants flower, but the vast majority do. Of the 287,655 known species, 258,650 flower. The remainder are Bryophytes such as moss and hornworts.

? how many beer bottles from earth to mars

Mars can be up to 399,000,000 km from Earth. A beer bottle is 24 cm high, so it would take 1,662,500,000,000 beer bottles to reach Mars.

? if you put all the sheep in scotland end to end, how far would they reach

AQA estimates that if you put all the sheep in Scotland end to end the line would stretch for 8,000 km. You'd need 160,000 sheepdogs to keep them in line.

? is there anything darker than black

Scientifically black is not a colour. Black absorbs all the colours of the visible spectrum and reflects none of them, so nothing is darker than black.

? what colour is water

Water is very slightly blue. This colour only becomes visible at depths of at least 3 metres. Thus the sea does not reflect the sky, as is commonly thought.

how many dentists does it take to put out a fire

It takes one dentist and huge amounts of vile pink mouthwash to put out a fire – but you have to make an appointment three weeks in advance and the bill is huge.

if i was strap 100 pencils together, how long would it take to count to one billion through the tally system

Assuming you tallied at the rate of 1 stroke per second, with 100 pencils you'd reach 1 billion in 115 days, 17 hours, 46 minutes and 40 seconds.

who invented the graph

Economist William Playfair published the first data graphs in 1876, but mathematician James Joseph Sylvester first introduced the term 'graph' in 1878.

celebrity q&a

iain lee

who is iain lee

The tall, lanky, pale guy from the *11 O'Clock Show* and *Rise*. He likes The Monkees, The Beach Boys and he's good to his mum. And his cat, Velvet.

what's the meaning of life

Listen to as much great music as you can, try as many different things as possible, even naughty things, don't hurt people and try and be as nice as you can.

if you could be any character from the series 'lost' for a day, who would it be and why

I would be Tom. He's the Other that used to wear a beard, but doesn't. It turns out he's quite dumb and cowardly, and that excites me.

? you were brought up in
slough. i've never been. is it
as bad as ricky gervais from
'the office' says it is

> I don't think he said it was especially
> bad, did he? Maybe he did in the
> second series, I missed that one. It's
> alright. I'm there every week doing
> the shopping for my mum, so I have
> to be careful what I say.

? you are a fan of kiss – is it
their music or fashion sense
that appeals

> I got into them in an ironic way,
> attracted by the ridiculous make-up
> and outrageous stories. Turned out
> though, that their early music was
> just fantastic. Once they got into the
> 80s and took off their make-up, they
> became awful.

? was it an accident or good
planning that you were
born on the same day as
johnny depp

> You'd have to ask my mum. It is
> amazing how similar our careers have
> been.

9

what percentage of cars on the road are red?

On the road – commuting, travel and holidays

which ship has the largest number of seats in its permanent on-board cinema

The ship *Queen Elizabeth 2 (QE2)* has the largest cinema at sea with a capacity of 531. She cost just over £29 million to build in 1969.

which form of everyday transport is spelled the same in french, english, german and swedish

Taxi is spelled exactly the same in English, French, German, Swedish, Portuguese, and Dutch. Horse-drawn carriages (taxis) started in the 17th century.

statistically which of the major countries has the safest air travel over the past 20 years

Australian airline QANTAS has never had a fatal accident, and is the safest. QANTAS = Queensland & Northern Territory Aerial Service.

which country has the highest car crash rate in europe

Greece has the highest car accident rate in Europe. The Republic of Ireland has Europe's highest rate of fatalities caused by car accidents.

why isn't the rotherhithe tunnel straight

The Rotherhithe Tunnel was built with bends so that horses would not be able to see the light at the other end and bolt for the exit.

how many people from the uk will have a holiday in august

About 44% of British plan their holiday for August. September and July appear to be the next favourite months with 46%. August is the world favourite.

? when having your air conditioning on in the car does this use extra petrol or is it just a myth

It is partly true: at less than 50 mph it is more fuel efficient to leave your windows down, but over 50 mph, air conditioning is more fuel efficient.

? what percentage of cars on the road are red

Of the 26 million UK cars, the colours are: silver/grey, 36%; black/dark grey, 24%; blue, 18%; red, 11%; white, 6%; green, 3%; yellow, 2%; pink, 0.02%.

? why is the lower part of trees in greece painted white please

The white paint on trees in Greece acts firstly as an insect repellent and secondly as a way to reflect light at night on the country's badly lit roads.

? why should people in sheffield driving ford orions be worried

Car owners in Sheffield are five times more likely to have their car stolen than any other residents in the country. Ford Orions are the most popular target.

? what is the highest capital city in the world

La Paz, the administrative capital of Bolivia, is the highest capital city in the world with an altitude of 11,811 ft. 'La Paz' means 'The Peace'.

? what's the longest time anyone has been stuck in a lift for

Cypriot Kively Papajohn, then 76, got stuck in an elevator on 28 December 1987. It was not until six days later that she finally got out.

? name 10 tube stations on one line that start with same letter

On the Piccadilly Line, Heathrow T4; Heathrow T1, 2, 3; Hatton Cross; Hounslow West; Hounslow Central; Hounslow East; Hammersmith; Hyde Park Corner; Holborn; Holloway Road.

? do chinese mobile phones have mandarin keypads

Chinese mobiles do not have Mandarin characters but use algorithms to translate keystrokes into Mandarin, or recognise characters written on the screen.

? can you tell me the best way to get to mexico if you are afraid of flying and you live in aylesbury

Leave Southampton on the *QE2* to New York, cruise to Los Angeles via Mexico, get the train to New York, then get the *QE2* home. Round trip of 29 days.

? you sail a boat, you fly a plane, what do you do with a submarine when it is submerged

When a submarine is submerged you would say that you are 'driving' it. The first military submarine was called the *Turtle*, built in 1775.

? how are friday 9 january 1863 and the london tube related

On Friday 9 January 1863, the first section of the London Underground Railway opened between Paddington and Farringdon Street; the map marks this date.

? are men better drivers

No, women are safer. An Automobile Association survey found men drive faster and break the law more often than women. Men are more likely to be killed.

? i'm with a man who claims to have been brought to our time by a time traveller. he wants to get back to feudal england. how can he do it & when will it be possible

It depends on his mode of transport into 2007. It's possible he will struggle with Sunday services. There's a 23 bus to AD 420 tomorrow at 7.30 am.

? what is the largest roundabout in europe

The Arc de Triomphe in France is Europe's largest traffic roundabout, and the meeting point of twelve avenues. No vehicle insurance policy is valid on it.

? name 3 things that have been left on the moon by nasa

Three things which have been left on the moon by NASA are a footprint, a 'lunar laser ranging retroreflector array' and an Apollo 17 commemorative plaque.

? how big is london waterloo train station

Waterloo's main structure is a 1,200-foot-long steel and glass tube that tapers from a width of 150 ft to 105 ft. It has 19 platforms.

? what is weakest currency in the world

The weakest currency in the world is the Zimbabwean dollar, as the African nation has the highest inflation in the world at over 1,000%.

? how long would it take to walk to china and back

The distance London–Beijing is 5,070 miles, so 10,140 on a round trip. Walking speed 4 mph; 2,535 hours walking time; 8 hrs walking per day: 316.8 days.

? how many tyres would u need 2 stack on top of each other 2 reach the moon

The distance to the moon varies between 356,410 and 406,740 km while tyres stack at 5 to a metre. You will need 1.782 to 2.034 billion tyres and long arms.

? which countries drive on the left-hand side of the road

There are 75 countries that drive on the left including Australia, the UK, the Bahamas, Bangladesh, Barbados, Bermuda, Botswana, Cyprus, Ireland and Malta.

? how many taxis are there in london

There are 21,000 black cab taxis in London (taking 85 million fares per year, mostly in London and around Heathrow) and 40,000 minicabs.

**? in las vegas for every 8
people there is one what**

There is one slot machine in Las
Vegas for every eight people who live
there. Elvis Presley performed 837
consecutive sold-out shows at the Las
Vegas Hilton.

**? how many beds are there if
you count up every bed in
every room in every hilton
hotel in the world**

There are 221,500 beds in the world's
Hilton hotels. If laid end to end, they
would stretch for 272 miles. Conrad
Hilton founded the company in 1919.

? when was the m3 opened

The M3 motorway opened in stages as
follows: J1 to J3, 1974; J3 to J8, 1971;
J8 to J10, 1985; J10 to J14, 1995. The
motorway is 59 miles long.

what is the longest tube in london

The longest journey without a train change on the London Underground is on the Central Line from West Ruislip to Epping (34.1 miles).

in relation to seafaring, what is st elmo's fire

St Elmo's Fire is a bright blue-purple glow in the sky, often during thunderstorms, held to be a good omen for sailors. St Elmo is the patron saint of sailors.

how much horse power has the channel tunnel train got

Eurostar's distinctive aerodynamic-looking trains weigh in at 800 tonnes each and generate 16,408 bhp – roughly the power of twenty Formula One racing cars.

alain de botton

who is alain de botton

A writer trying to answer some of the big but everyday questions of life in a clear, elegant and entertaining way.

is it better to travel hopefully than to arrive

Happiness is mostly derived from pursuing a goal. As soon as you've achieved it, within fifteen minutes, the mind starts to get restless for a new challenge.

who would win in a fight between marcel proust and soren kierkegaard

Proust would immediately surrender and try to charm Kierkegaard by telling him how much he had enjoyed his work. In that way, surreptitiously, he would win.

? which experiment could provide the most important philosophical answers to humanity, regardless of practicality and/or morality

It would be fascinating to run experiments about how much nature and nurture influence upbringing. You could try out educating the same child in a number of different ways and plot the results.

? what is beauty

Beauty is a material version of what we call 'good' more generally. Beauty is also a promise of happiness.

? do you think being called bert grimes would have set you on a different career path? if so, what

Under that name, I would almost certainly have followed my alternative career path: to be an architect. Grimes has a solid sounding name that would be a perfect way to reassure clients.

what is the most unpopular sport in the world?

The sports locker

? **was colin montgomerie ever world number one**

> Colin Montgomerie was never ranked no. 1. He first reached the top ten in the Official World Golf Rankings in 1994 and was ranked no. 3 at his peak.

? **has there ever been a hole in one at the ryder cup**

> The six golfers to have made hole in ones in the Ryder Cup are: Peter Butler, Nick Faldo, Costantino Rocca, Howard Clark, Scott Verplank and Paul Casey.

? **who has captained england the most times in any sport**

> Bobby Moore has captained England the most, the sport being football. He won 108 caps, with 90 of those as captain, including the 1966 World Cup final.

which footballer was brought on to replace his dad in an international

Eidur Gudjohnsen became the first player to replace his father (Arnor) in an international match, when Iceland faced Estonia in 1996. They won 3–0.

what do john lennon and gary lineker have in common

Both John Lennon and Gary Lineker have the middle name Winston; named after Winston Churchill. Lineker shares a birthday with Churchill on 30 November.

who has recently designed a nineteen hole golf course

Colin Montgomerie has designed a course with 19 holes at Rowallan, in Ayrshire. If the game is a tie, the 19th hole will be used as the decider.

what is the most played sport in the world

The most played sport in the world is football, which is enjoyed by 1,002 million people. This is followed by volleyball, which is played by 998 million.

which teams still in the football league are older than aston villa

Football League teams older than Aston Villa are Chesterfield, Notts County, Notts Forest, Stoke City, Reading, Rotherham, Sheffield Weds and Wrexham.

what is the name of the american football player who held the record for the longest field goal although he only had half a foot

Tom Dempsey was born with no toes on his right foot and still holds the record for the longest field goal in American football (63 yards), scored in 1970.

? who played in the first fa cup final

> The first FA Cup Final was in 1872 between Wanderers and Royal Engineers. Wanderers won 1–0. It was played at the Kennington Oval to a crowd of 2,000.

? why do so many spanish football clubs have crowns as part of their club badges

> Several Spanish clubs were given royal patronage, such as RCD Español, which allowed them to use 'Real' as a prefix and the crown on their badges.

? who founded rangers football club

> Moses McNeil, his brother Peter and two friends founded GRFC. Moses suggested the name Rangers in 1872 after seeing the name in a book about English Rugby.

only british player to be top scorer in italy's serie a

The only British player to win the Capocannonieri (Serie A top scorer) is the great Welshman John Charles, who scored 28 goals in 1957/58 for Juventus.

who has played for and against england, for and against liverpool and for and against everton

Dave Watson played for Liverpool and Everton, and against both teams for Norwich. He won twelve caps for England and one against for the Hong Kong Golden Select XI.

who holds the record for the most consecutive clean sheets in the football league not the premiership

Steve Death of Reading holds the record for the most consecutive clean sheets in the Football League, with 26 in 1978/9. Reading were then in Division 4.

❓ who's the fattest wrestler

The world's heaviest wrestler ever is Hawaiian sumo wrestler Konishiki, who weighs 41.5 stone (264 kilos). Konishiki's nickname is 'The Dump Truck'.

❓ what is the most unpopular sport in the world

In a recent poll, 81% of respondents said dog fighting is the most unpopular sport. Corrida (bullfighting) and fox hunting were second and third.

❓ how many miles is the record for walking with a milk bottle balanced on the head

The greatest distance walked by a person continuously balancing a milk bottle on the head is 130.3 km (80.96 miles) by Ashrita Furman of New York, USA.

? what is the weirdest sport in the world

Bog snorkelling is the weirdest sport in the world. It involves swimming through a 60-yard trench in a peat bog. Synchronised swimming is a close second.

? what is the most number of people that have won the national lottery jackpot in england at any one time

The highest number of people to win the National Lottery jackpot at any one time is 133. The draw on 14 November 1995 saw 133 tickets share £16 million.

? what was the least number of horses to finish in a grand national

The least number of horses to finish the Grand National was two horses. This was in 1928, when it saw the record number of 42 horses start the race.

? when and what was the first football-like sport played and who invented football

Cujo was a ball sport played by the ancient Chinese in the fifth century BC. Volleyball was invented in 1895 by William G. Morgan.

? what is the world record for the largest amount in kg of belly button fluff

Graham Barker of Tuart Hill, Western Australia, has collected 15.41g of his own navel fluff since 1984. He started collecting in a 'bored moment'.

? what is in a golf ball

A golf ball has a titanium-based, pressurised core that is located under 3–4 layers of synthetic material. In the 1600s they contained goose feathers.

where did the term bogey derive from in the game of golf

The term 'bogey' derives from a match played in 1890 wherein a Major Wellman called his opponent, Dr Thomas Browne, a 'bogey-man' because of the ground score system.

who were the youngest and oldest winners of the us masters golf

The youngest person to win the US Masters is Tiger Woods, in 1997, when he was just 21 years old. Jack Nicklaus became the oldest winner in 1986 at 46.

which is the only non league football team to win the fa cup

Tottenham Hotspur is the only non league football team to win the FA Cup, beating Sheffield United 3–1 in 1901. Spurs were a non-league side at the time.

how many people have played for england who have the letter x in their surname

Thirteen players have Xs: J. Cox, J. D. Cox, R. Dix, J. Dixon, K. Dixon, L. Dixon, M. Duxbury, F. Fox, G. Le Saux, G. Molyneux, A. Quixall, G. Rix, J. Wilcox.

how many tampons would it take to completely drain an olympic size swimming pool

An Olympic swimming pool holds around 2.5 million litres and a tampon 3.04 ml, so it'd take 822,368,422 tampons to drain the pool.

what player in the premiership history had the most obscure name

Orfeo Keizerweerd (Oldham) had the most obscure name in the Premiership. Honourable mentions to Shane Cansdell-Sherriff, Jelle Van Damme and Boaz Myhill.

the 1911 ladies final at wimbledon lasted how many minutes

> Dorothea Lambert Chambers thrashed Dora Boothby 6–0, 6–0 in the 1911 Wimbledon Ladies' Final. The one-sided match lasted for a total of 25 minutes.

who was john mcenroe playing at wimbledon when he famously yelled you cannot be serious at the referee

> John McEnroe's 'You cannot be serious' phrase was first famously yelled during his first round Wimbledon match against Tom Gullikson in 1981.

which is the largest golf course in the world

> The world's longest golf course is Jade Dragon Snow Mountain Golf Club, Lijiang City, China, measuring 8,450 yards, par 72, including a 735-yard par 5.

when was conkers first played

The first recorded game of conkers using horse chestnuts was on the Isle of Wight in 1848. Until then, children used snail shells or hazelnuts.

when the game of polo was first invented, could you play it both right and left handed

Polo originated in Central Asia around 2,500 years ago, and was played any way you liked. Left-handed play was only banned, for safety reasons, in 1975.

what was the year that the england football team first started wearing their names on the back of their shirts

Names first appeared on the back of England footballers' shirts in 1992. Numbers first appeared in 1937, when England lost 3–1 to Scotland.

? has richard hammond broken a world record for the fastest car crash survived

Richard Hammond doesn't hold the world record for the fastest survived car crash. Craig Breedlove crashed at around 675 mph on 28 October 1996 and survived.

? when did the first gym open

The first modern gym was one built for children in Hesse, Germany, in 1852 by Adolph Spiess. The Greek word gymnasium means 'place to be naked'.

? is it true there is an ancient law banning football

Yes. Between 1324 and 1667, football was banned in England by more than thirty royal and local laws because it was unruly and distracted people from archery.

what is shirling

Shirling is a game in which two teams of five form a circle around a snake, trying to pull each other in front of the snake and provoke it into biting them.

what is the highest height any horse has jumped

The world record for puissance (horse high jump) is 8 ft 1.25 in (2.47 m). It was set in Chile on 5 February 1949 by Alberto Larraguibel riding Huaso.

why does bruce grobbelaar write the numbers 1 3 1 3 beneath his autograph

Zimbabwean goalkeeper Bruce Grobbelaar writes '13 13' beneath his autograph because he played for Liverpool for 13 years, winning 13 major trophies.

? who has scored for both teams in an fa cup final

In the 1981 FA Cup final Manchester City's Tommy Hutchinson scored a goal and an own goal. Tottenham's Gary Mabbutt repeated this in 1987. Bert Turner did it in 1946.

? why is roulette known as the devil's game

Roulette is sometimes called the Devil's Game because the numbers add up to 666, but it undeniably has a diabolical hold on some people.

? what sport was banned in scotland during the middle ages in favour of archery

In 1457, golf was banned in Scotland because it interfered with the practice of archery. In defiance, it was played on seaside courses called links.

? who was the last player with a moustache to score a goal for england? own goals and david beckham's facial hair don't count

The last player with just a moustache to score for England was Viv Anderson, in a European Championships Qualifier against Yugoslavia on 12 November 1986.

? what stopped inches short of the finishing line in a south africa race, costing its owner £2,500

Gorky the pigeon stopped inches short in a 400-mile race, allowing Feathers to enter the loft first in Pietermaritzburg, South Africa, and win £2,500.

? if a footballer earns £100,000 a week, how much does he earn every time he breathes in and out

The average person breathes 12 times a minute; 10,080 minutes in a week; that's 120,960 breaths. So someone earning £100,000 per week earns 82p per breath.

? name footballers with fishy names

Footballers with fishy sounding names: John Scales, Sol Campbell, Bert Trout-man, Sting-ray Wilkins, Sardine Saunders, Mark Fish, Ledley King Prawn.

? how many world-title boxers retired with 0 losses

The unbeaten World Champion Rocky Marciano won all 49 of his professional fights, with 43 knockouts. He defended his World Heavyweight title six times.

which footballer has the fastest shot and how fast was it

The hardest shot ever recorded was David Hirst's 14.8 yard, 114 mph shot for Sheffield Wednesday in 1996. It hit the crossbar and Arsenal won 4–1.

who was first foreigner to captain an fa cup winning team

Eric Cantona was the first foreigner to captain an FA Cup winning team, for Manchester United in the 1996 FA Cup win against Liverpool.

what weighs 4 ounces that you throw in sports

The only ball that weighs 4 oz is a women's (from $4^{15}/_{16}$ oz) or youth's ($4^{11}/_{16}$ oz) cricket ball. Men's cricket balls weigh from $5^{1}/_{2}$ oz.

who was the first footballer not to wear standard black and white football boots in a competitive game

The first player not to wear black and white boots was Alan Ball in 1970. He had old Adidas boots painted white to pretend they were his new Hummel ones.

what is the most goals scored by a keeper in a game of football

Jose Chilavert is the only keeper ever to score a hat-trick in a competitive game when playing as a keeper. Jose scored a total of 62 competitive goals.

could you give me the details of the occasion when w g grace was clean bowled but refused to walk, particularly the line he apparently said to the bowler

W. G. Grace was bowled out on the first ball of a charity match, but continued to play, exclaiming, 'They came to see me bat, not to see you umpire.'

? is it true a horse was disqualified from winning a race for eating a mars bar

The horse No Bombs won by 8 lengths at Ascot in 1979, but was disqualified when caffeine and theobromine, from a Mars Bar, were found in its blood test.

? how many hits of a golf ball would it take tiger woods to get from milton keynes to nigeria

Tiger Woods regularly drives the ball 300 yards, so it would take 18,457 shots to travel the 3,146 miles from Milton Keynes to Lagos in Nigeria.

? when was the first football made

Charles Goodyear produced the first vulcanised rubber soccer ball in 1855. Prior to this, balls were dependent on the size and shape of the pig's bladder.

? do more people have heart attacks while england are in a penalty shoot out than normal

Recent studies have shown that heart attacks increase by 25% on the day, and for two days after an England penalty shoot out, shown by the 1998 Argentina loss.

? name the players maradona took the ball round to score against england in 1986

Diego Maradona beat six England players to score the Goal of the Century: Glenn Hoddle, Peter Reid, Kenny Sansom, Terry Butcher, Terry Fenwick, and Peter Shilton.

? which english football club has 5 r's in its name

Kidderminster Harriers is the English football club with five rs in its name. They were founded in 1886 and play at the Aggborough Stadium.

? which is bigger in proportion, a tennis ball to a tennis court or a football to a football pitch

A 260.86 sq m tennis court is 81,090 times bigger than a tennis ball, whereas a 6,300 sq m football pitch is 161,567 times bigger than a football.

? how much does beckham earn a second

David Beckham will earn US$1 million a week signed to Los Angeles Galaxy, which equates to just over $1.65 per second, even when he's asleep.

? how many times do you have to win the european cup before you keep it

If a team wins the European Cup three times in a row they get to keep it. If they win it five times they also get to keep it. Liverpool received theirs in 2005.

? who was first heavyweight champion of the world

John L Sullivan was the first Heavyweight Champion of the World under modern rules. He was born in Roxbury, Massachusetts. He beat Paddy Ryan in 1882.

? what is the longest penalty shoot-out

The longest penalty shoot-out took 48 penalties, and was between KK Palace and Civics in the NFA cup, 23 January 2005. The score was 17–16.

? what is a button boy in golf

The Button Boys were a group of young golfers signed by Ernest Button, a wealthy businessman, in the 1960s and given top class training to win tournaments.

katie puckrik

? who is katie puckrik

I'm a TV presenter and a writer. I'm also a dancer, singer and cupcake eater. I've been called a 'very funny lady' by the late Barry White, which has no credibility, since he was only the Walrus of Love, not the Manatee of Laughs.

? what's the meaning of life

There is no intrinsic meaning to life. Life just 'is', and we're along for the ride, with all the other critters. But we can always take a stab at improving matters while we're here by respecting the dignity of others and ourselves.

? what's your funniest joke

Where do you find a dog with no legs? Right where you left him.

? what's the best bargain you ever bought

My old flat in Maida Vale. It was on the top two floors of a council block and had a picture-postcard view of London.

? you were in a short-lived band in the mid-80s called puck. the spice girls, take that and even the verve are reforming. will we see a comeback from puck

For the habitués of London's old dive bars and gay clubs, a fevered memory shall have to suffice of me with my red beehive, nerd glasses and brothel creepers, singing at the top of my lungs to backing tracks while twirling nine inflatable dogs over my head and dancing like Ann-Margret on meth.

what is the weirdest known phobia?

Etymology, origins and debunking myths

? what is the weirdest pub name

The weirdest pub name is Poosie Nansie's, but there are many: Sally Up Steps; Donkey on Fire; Oxnoble; Who'd A Thowt It; Tafarn Sinc; and the shortest – Q.

? where does the term 'fired' originate in an employment sense

The original term was 'fire out' (1871), meaning eject or throw someone out. It was shortened to 'fired' (1885), perhaps helped by the 'discharge' link.

? in rhyming slang a douglas hird is a third degree, at uni, a desmond tutu is a 2.2, but what is a 2.1 in slang?

Degree rhyming slang: 1st – Geoff (Hurst), Damien (Hirst); 2:1 – Attila (the Hun), Don (Juan); 2:2 – Desmond (Tutu); 3rd – Douglas (Hurd), Thora (Hird).

why are we called great britain & what is the meaning of the name great

Great Britain is the largest, hence 'great', island of the British Isles. Strictly speaking 'we' are the United Kingdom of Great Britain and Northern Ireland, or UK for short.

what does lego mean in english

LEGO comes from Danish 'leg godt', meaning 'play well'. The company adopted the name in 1934 and it was later realised that in Latin it means 'I assemble'.

what is the etymological root of the word adultery

The word 'adultery' comes from the Middle English alteration of 'avoutrie' from the Anglo-French 'avulterie', which in turn came from the Latin 'adulterium'.

? why is the peace symbol upside down, i thought it would be the other way up to replicate the two fingered salute

Gerald Holtom designed the CND symbol in 1958. He said it incorporated the semaphore N and D, and showed a person in despair, arms down, palms outstretched.

? how many different family surnames are there in the uk

There are approximately 1.38 million different surnames divided between an estimated 60.78 million UK residents. That's one surname for every 44 people.

? what month is the earth closest to the sun

Earth is nearest the sun (perihelion) in January and furthest away (aphelion) in July. The dates vary: in 2008, 3 January is the perihelion and 4 July the aphelion.

? what is a copper bottom investment

In slang, a thing that's copper-bottomed is certain, especially financially. It originates from the practice of applying copper to the bottom of a ship.

? what are foreman and lechman old terms for

Foreman, longman, lechman, littleman and thuma are the old terms for the fingers: index, middle, ring, little and thumb respectively.

? where did the saying no strings attached come from

Cloth merchants mark flaws in cloth with a tiny white string. Flawless cloth is still ordered on Savile Row today by requesting 'no strings attached'.

? **there are 3 six letter words
in the english language
with their letters in
alphabetical order without
repetition, what are they**

The three six-letter words with letters
in alphabetical order without
repetition are 'abhors', 'almost' and
'biopsy'. 'Sponged' and 'wronged'
(seven letters) are in reverse order.

? **what 8-letter word means
practices or beliefs of little
worth**

Practices or beliefs of little worth
could be 'nonsense' or 'malarkey' or
'tommyrot' or 'claptrap' – words not
normally associated with AQA
answers.

**? think of a word, any word –
such that taking away the
first and last letter leaves
you with one more than the
number of letters in the
original word. what is it**

If you take away the first and last
letters of the seven-letter words
'weighty' or 'heights', you are left
with 'eight', which is one more than
seven.

? how many is a few

Most consider a few to be less than
several and therefore certainly less
than some. But it's more than two,
since two is definitely a couple. So
three or four.

**? what is the difference
between flotsam and jetsam**

Jetsam are goods voluntarily cast into
the sea (jettisoned), whereas flotsam
are goods floating on the water that
have not been thrown in deliberately.

what is the fear of cheese

The fear of cheese is turophobia; love of cheese is turophilia. In 1878, using 54 Stilton cheeses, Tom Nuttall made a 60ft replica of Cleopatra's Needle.

why do they call it a hat trick when a footballer scores three times

The term 'hat trick' originated from cricket, where a hat or cap was customarily given to a bowler who achieved the feat of taking three wickets in a row.

there is one 9 letter word in the english alphabet, from which you can take away one letter at a time and get another word. what is it

You can keep removing a letter from the word 'startling', forming new words along the way: 'startling', 'starting', 'staring', 'string', 'sting', 'sing', 'sin', 'in', 'I'.

what is the scientific name for someone with a fear of the colour green

There's no word for a phobia of green, but prasinophobia would work well. Other fears: chromophobia (colours); leukophobia (white); and melanophobia (black).

why is a pint called a pint

The word pint is derived from the Latin 'picta' meaning painted – referring to a painted mark on a vessel indicating measure. A pint is 1/8 of a gallon.

why in the marriage ceremony does the bride stand on the left side as u look at the altar

The tradition of the bride standing on the left harks back to times when the groom would have to keep his sword hand free to fight off other suitors.

? what is the meaning behind each of the days of the week and where did the words come from

The days of the week, Sunday to Saturday, are named after: the sun; the moon; the Norse gods Tyr, Woden (Odin), Thor and Frigg; and the Roman god Saturn.

? why is cider called cider

The origin of 'cider' is thought to be 'sagara', the Basque word for apple tree. Also the Latin is 'sicera', Hebrew 'shekhar', French 'cidre' and Greek 'sikera'.

? where does the expression graveyard shift come from

The graveyard shift was coined in the 1800s, when graveyard attendants worked night shifts to be alert for 'waking corpses' who had been buried alive.

what's the origin of the phrase got the hump as in you have got the hump

Some believe 'got the hump' comes from Mr Punch, who stored his troubles in one, but it's more likely to hail from the slouch of an exasperated person.

origin of phrase on the lam

'Lam' as in 'on the lam' derives from an Icelandic word 'lemje' meaning 'beat'. The implication is that the feet are beating the ground hard while running.

where does the term freelancing come from and what is its meaning

The original 'free lancers' were medieval mercenary soldiers. The word still refers to those offering their (usually less violent) services where needed.

why is it that when doctors get a specialty they get called mr whatever not doctor whatever?

Medicine and surgery were once separate professions: physicians went to university and became Dr; surgeons learned on the job and became master tradesmen and Mr.

where does the word umbrella come from

Umbrella comes from the Latin 'umbra', meaning shade or shadow. AQA prefers the term 'brolly', but the French have it spot on with 'parapluie'.

what is the origin of the word tit as in blue tit, great tit etc

'Tit' is an old Germanic word for 'small' and is used in many European languages. In Norway, 'titta' is used to describe a little girl.

what is a name for a young lamb

A very young lamb is called a 'slink'. An unweaned lamb is called a 'sucker'. A 'hoggett' is too old to be a lamb, but too young to be mutton.

what's the best number in the world

Phi is the best number (1.618, etc), mixing beauty and power, unless you're on a UK mobile network, when 63336 is best, providing answers to everything.

why is it called a wee when you urinate

The word 'wee', meaning to urinate, comes from the Middle English 'we', meaning 'little bit', and from the Old English for move or weigh: 'wegan'.

why do people say cobblers when they believe something isn't true

The British expression 'cobblers', meaning nonsense or rubbish, derives from 'cobbler's awls', Cockney rhyming slang for 'balls' (testicles).

who drew the pictures of the queen on the ten pound notes

In the 1960s, Harry Eccleston designed the Queen's portrait on UK banknotes. The current portrait on post-1993 notes is a modification by Andrew Ward.

what is the origin and meaning of the saying what the dickens

Dickens is a synonym for devil, originating in Tudor times from the nickname of Richard II ('Dickon'), who was hated by the Tudors for being a murderer.

why is new york called the big apple

New York was called 'The Big Apple' in the 1920s as horses were rewarded with apples on its many race tracks. A 1971 official tourism campaign used the expression.

what is the art of canal barge walking called

'Legging' is the name for walking a canal boat. It is done by lying on a plank balanced on the deck and using the feet to progress the boat through tunnels.

is there a collective noun for people in their 50th decade

A person who is fifty years old, or in his or her fifties, is called a quinquagenarian. The term has its roots in the Latin 'quinquaginta', meaning fifty.

how many words in the english language begin with su and sound like sh

> Two. George Bernard Shaw was asked if he knew that 'sugar' was the only word in the English language where 'su' was pronounced 'sh'. He replied, 'Sure.'

what is it called when you say words like kettle like kekkle

> Paralalia is a speech disorder marked by substitution of letters, e.g. kekkle for kettle. Rhoatism is the inability to pronounce 'r', like Jonathan Ross.

what is this sentence – i+opposite of w+initial of ice+double the letter b4t+3/4x +(1-1)+topless o

> The sentence spells out 'I miss you.' M is the opposite of W. I is the initial of ice. S is before T. 3/4 of X is Y. 1-1 is O. A topless O is U.

? where does the word limelight come from

Limelight originates from the burning of lime to create a strong light, used by lighthouses and the Victorian stage before the era of electric light.

? please tell me the derivation of spitalfield as in the marketplace etc

The name Spitalfields is a contraction of the name 'hospital fields' after a medieval hospital that existed there. The market was founded in 1638.

? which word in the english language has the most definitions

'Set' has the most definitions at 464. Run is 2nd at 396; go is 3rd (368); take 4th (343); stand 5th (334); get 6th (289); turn 7th (288); put 8th (268); fall 9th (264); and strike 10th (250).

? in the motorcycle world what is a minger

In motorcycle terms, a 'minger' is a wheelie. A 'mono' is also a wheelie. A 'war horse' is a well-ridden, road-worn bike, and 'pads' are tyres.

? what does g g g g u k 4 g g stand for

Gggguk4gg stands for 'A horse! A horse! My kingdom for a horse!' To help explain this, gg (gee-gee) is short for horse, with UK as the kingdom.

? how many people with the surname kettle are there in england

There are currently 3,027 people with the surname Kettle in the UK. Including the electrical appliances, there are currently 68,962,227 kettles in the UK.

? with the exception of royalty who was the first woman on british banknotes

Other than royalty, the first woman on a British banknote was Florence Nightingale in the 1970s (unless goddesses count, in which case it was Britannia).

? what is the commonest word in the english language

The most common word in the English language is 'the'. Then in ascending order from 2 to 9 are: 'of', 'to', 'and', 'a', 'in', 'is', 'it', 'you' and 'that'.

? traditionally, the staircases in fire stations are spiral – why is this

Fire engines used to be horse drawn. The horses were kept on the ground floor of the station and spiral stairs were used to prevent them climbing upstairs.

?where did the phrase skulduggery originate from

> Skulduggery, meaning cheating or misrepresentation, derives from the Scottish term 'sculdudrie', which meant adultery – also a type of cheating.

?what are the left-over pieces of paper from a hole punch called

> The small pieces of paper generated by hole punches are called 'chads' or 'chips'. The word chad became famous after the 2000 US presidential election.

?when did the line to love, honour and obey become optional in the wedding vows

> The word 'obey' in a bride's wedding promise was made optional in 1928 (the Series I Marriage Service). Lady Diana was the first royal not to include it.

what is the prong of a fork called

The prongs on forks are called tines. An Italian invention, forks were at first viewed with curiosity. There are now over twenty types of dining fork used.

why is it medieval and not medigood

The word 'medieval' is from the Latin 'medium aevum' ('middle age'). While the period is often referred to as the 'Dark Ages', it does not mean evil.

where does the term purple patch originate

A 'purple patch', describing a period of success and good form, derives from Roman times, when only noblemen could afford purple dyes and cloth.

why is the end of may a bank holiday

The last Monday in May is known in the Christian calendar as Pentecost or Whitsun. It celebrates the day the apostles were blessed by the Holy Spirit.

what is the strangest religion in the world and why

The strangest religion in the world is 'Jedi'. Thousands of people listed it as their religion on 2001 census forms, even though it's from *Star Wars*.

what is franmas and when is it celebrated

Franmas was established in 1997 in the south-east of England. It is held in celebration of Francesca the Fairy on the closest Sunday to 14 June.

？what is the weirdest known phobia

There are over 700 known phobias.
AQA thinks one of the weirdest ones
is hippopotomonstrosesquippedaliophobia,
which is the fear of long words.

？why do we say two cents

'My two cents' refers to your opinion.
By minimising 'my opinion' to the
value of 'my two cents', the possibility
of offending another is avoided.

？where did the phase 'tits up' come from

Early navigation systems on aircraft
were designed to turn upside down
when not working so as not to
confuse pilots. When so, they
resembled breasts.

can you answer these?

We hope you've been so impressed, entertained, and astounded by this second volume of questions and answers that you've saved 63336 in your phone for later.

Now it's your turn to impress us. From time to time we get the odd question that stumps us. Despite hours of searching, pondering and discussion there's a few questions out there that we still haven't been able to answer. Can you help us out? We'll be eternally grateful and, who knows, there may even be a job open for you. Some of the toughest are on the next page. Answers in an email, please, to hello@aqa.63336.com.

? what connects rainbow warrior, westminster abbey, eiffel tower and blackadder

? what have the following got in common: guinness, the bee gees, one foot in the grave and carling

? clue, time to choose, time to play. which male celebrity

? i was old before i was young, i'm in a story that was never told. what am i

? can u solve this riddle? what has 6 arms, 11 legs, 2 heads, and it's round

? what is lean, green, round and a living machine in your living room

? ditloid: O 8 T O A S O what is the answer

? what is 100 z of q

? i live in the sea but cannot swim, fly but cannot land and eat but cannot sleep! what am i